THE
Novelist's
NOTEBOOK

LAURIE HENRY

STORY PRESS
CINCINNATI, OHIO

BIOGRAPHICAL SKETCH

Laurie Henry has graduate degrees in writing from Johns Hopkins University and the University of Iowa. She was a fellow at the Provincetown Fine Arts Work Center. Her book, *The Fiction Dictionary*, a compendium of terms and examples from literature, was published by Story Press in 1995. She teaches English at Raymond Walters College, a branch of the University of Cincinnati, and is associate editor of *Story* magazine. She is working on a novel.

This hardcover edition of **The Novelist's Notebook** features a "self-jacket" that eliminates the need for a separate dust jacket. It provides sturdy protection for your book while it saves paper, trees and energy.

Other fine Story Press Books are available from your local bookstore or direct from the publisher.

03   02   01   00   99   5   4   3   2   1

Library of Congress Cataloging in Publication Data

Henry, Laurie.
   The novelist's notebook / by Laurie Henry. – 1st ed.
      p.   cm.   4
   ISBN 1-884910-42-4 (hardcover : alk. paper)
    1. Fiction—Technique—Problems, exercises, etc.   I. Title.
PN3355.H466   1999
808.3—dc21   98-52050
                                 CIP

Designed by Clare Finney
Cover illustration: *Lament of the Lovers*, 1953 by Joan Miró. © 1999 Artists Rights Society (ARS), New York/ADAGP, Paris.

For John, Eric, and Becky

ACKNOWLEDGEMENTS

Thanks to Lois Rosenthal and Jack Heffron and others at Story Press for their guidance through the writing process. Thanks to John Drury, for his attention to detail as he read all of my rough drafts. Thanks to my fiction-writing teachers, especially Diane Vreuls, John Barth, Leonard Michaels, and Joy Williams for their wise words over the years. Thanks also to LaWanda Walters, David Serling, and Terry Stokes for their quiet inspiration.

Contents

Introduction

Writing a novel can be a lengthy process, and it's hard working alone. Think of *The Novelist's Notebook* as an encouraging companion who can assist you along the way. Turn to it when you're stuck or when you need to find focus. In these pages you can confide your hopes, your doubts, and celebrate your flashes of insight. The activities and exercises are designed to help you organize, enrich, and give shape to your novel, as well as to give you the motivation to keep going. Audition your characters. Draw pictures of them. Pit them against a ticking clock. Write a letter from one character to another. Experiment. Take risks. Enjoy.

The book is divided into six sections. The first two will be the most useful in the early stages of writing, or even before you've gotten anything on paper. The last section will benefit you most when a large part of the book is finished. Start at the first page and work through to the end or skip around; do whichever activities capture your fancy or appeal to the mood you're in. And don't feel constrained by the space provided in the book. If you need more room, staple or clip on extra pages. Add pictures and photocopies important to your research. By the time you finish your novel, this book should be dog-eared—and a lot thicker.

Writers I've quoted in the book are novelists, and their work should be easy to find at bookstores or libraries. If a common thread runs through their advice—and mine—it's that to finish a novel, the most important step is to begin. I hope *The Novelist's Notebook* will help make the steps in what can be a long process easier, quicker, and more fun.

Planning

Why Me?

Imagine that a reader has just told a librarian at a large public library how much he loves your book and that he would like to read similar books by other writers. How would the librarian respond? Is there a specific classification to which your novel would belong? Is your work, for example, humorous literary fiction? Historical mystery? Erotic horror? Science fiction romance? Make your category as narrow as you'd like. After you've decided on your classification, think of a few other books you've read that belong in this category.

My novel belongs to the category of:_____

Other books that my readers might like:

_____ and _____

   Now spend a few paragraphs writing about what makes your book unique from other, similar books. Do you have special knowledge of the subject you're writing about? An unusual (or just unusually good) style? Is your outlook on your plot and characters exceptional in some way?

"Someone will always ask, 'How long does it take you to write a novel?' I hardly ever give them the real answer. 'It depends,' I will say. 'A year. Sometimes three or four.' The real answer, of course, is that it takes your entire life. I am forty-four, and it took me forty-four years to get this novel finished. You don't mention this to too many people, because it can fill their hearts with sadness, looking at you and thinking, Jesus, forty-four years to come up with *this*? But it's always the truest answer. You could not have written it any sooner. You write the book when its time has come, and you bring your lifetime to the task, however few or many years you have behind you."

—*James D. Houston*

What's Your Obsession?

List the subjects and themes you care about most—being a good parent, equal rights for all, preserving old houses, paying off credit cards—whatever they may be. Your list can also include the people and places you find most absorbing.

Then ask yourself why these are the most important people and issues in your life. Are there subjects and themes that recur in all the fiction you write? In several of Margaret Atwood's novels, for example, there is a male character who exposes himself to the young female protagonist. Will the most important themes in your real life be present in your novel?

Eudora Welty believes that no writer really chooses his subject. "It's not really quibbling," she writes, "to say that a writer's subject, in due time, chooses the writer—not of course *as* a writer, but as the man or woman who comes across it by living and has it to struggle with."

OBSESSION   **WHY?**

"Writers write about what obsesses them. You draw the cards. I lost my mother when I was 14. My daughter died at the age of 6. I lost my faith as a Catholic. When I'm writing, the darkness is always there. I go where the pain is." *—Anne Rice*

The Charged Image

Close your eyes and let your thoughts drift to your novel. What images come to you? What do your characters look like? When you think about these people, where are they? In a house? Outside? What does the atmosphere look like, sound like, smell like? What's going on? Are there particular objects, pieces of furniture, or books that take on a special importance?

The answers to these questions may help you define your novel's central images, what Joan Didion says "shimmer" for her when she writes. Most of these will probably be visual, but consider also sounds, odors, tastes, and tactile sensations. Now spend a few minutes writing about the pictures and other sensory images that come to you when you think about your novel. Write everything that comes to mind, no matter how vague or irrelevant the ideas might at first seem.

Now spend a few minutes reflecting on how these charged images relate to your work. Carole Maso, for example, began *Ghost Dance* when she was just twenty-one and "didn't know then what my concerns were, or what my obsessions were, and I had to write in order to find out." One day, she says, "an image appeared before me and that was of a very beautiful woman walking through the snow. Her feet are bright red and she has no idea that she feels cold. And I said, 'What's wrong with this woman?' and 'Where are the people who love her?' and 'Where is she going; what's happening?' and for three years I started writing around this image."

A dozen different writers, confronted with Maso's image of the barefoot woman in the snow, would come up with a dozen different novels to put her in. Thinking of the pictures in your mind, spend some time writing about some of the ways these images might influence your novel.

"Sometimes I'm sustained by a metaphor or an image. In *The Folded Leaf*, I knew that the suicide attempt was the climactic part of the novel but I didn't know how I was going to get there; the image that sustained me throughout the whole of the writing was that of walking across a very flat landscape toward the mountains; when I got to them, the necessary scenes would occur." —*William Maxwell*

Still Angry?

List the issues, both big and little, that make you mad. Include everything you can think of, from nuclear war to the guy who took the fifteen hundred dollars you gave him to reshingle the roof and spent it on a marijuana-buying trip to Jamaica.

Getting in touch with subjects you feel passionately about—negatively as well as positively—can help you decide what you need to write about. If you find most of the things on your list deal with being cheated out of money, for example, this may be an issue you want to explore in your novel. And while the goal here isn't therapy, after you've made your list, try to analyze what it says about you. Why did you, unlike anyone else in the world, trust this particular roofer with fifteen hundred dollars? If extreme gullibility is an issue in your life, perhaps a character who seems particularly gullible—even if your novel isn't autobiographical—would interest you. Or, it could simply be satisfying to include a character based on your crooked roofer (though see the libel warnings on page 24).

"I write because I hate. A lot. Hard." —*William Gass*

6

Reading List

List your ten favorite novels of all time, in order of preference. Include no more than two by any single author. Go to the library or bookstore if necessary, to remind yourself of works you may have forgotten. Then briefly write *why* the book is a favorite of yours and what, if anything, you can learn from it that will help you write your own novel.

FAVORITE NOVEL **WHY?**

1. _____   _____
                               _____

2. _____   _____
                               _____

3. _____   _____
                               _____

4. _____   _____
                               _____

5. _____   _____
                               _____

6. _____   _____
                               _____

7. _____   _____
                               _____

8. _____   _____
                               _____

9. _____   _____
                               _____

10. _____   _____
                               _____

To a young writer, William Faulkner urged: "Read, read, read. Read everything—trash, classics, good and bad, and see how they do it. Just like a carpenter who works as an apprentice and studies the master. Read! You'll absorb it. Then write. If it is good, you'll find out. If it's not, throw it out the window."

Rules and Expections

Does your novel belong to a genre that has specific rules? Or are there certain expectations your readers are likely to hold for the outcome of the plot?

A mystery, for example, is likely to include a crime, a perpetrator, clues, red herrings, and finally a solution. Even a literary novel has its conventions—for example, characters, some kind of plot, vivid scenes, and a conclusion that grows naturally from the interaction of characters and plot.

It's important to understand the rules and conventions of your kind of book before you decide to break them—but then you may decide to do just that. In Russell Hoban's *Turtle Diary*, a lonely, isolated man and woman share a desire to free two unhappy-looking zoo turtles. After the turtles are freed, the reader's expectation is that the human characters will then develop a more intimate personal relationship, but this doesn't happen. Instead, they return to their isolation, apparently unchanged. A single incident, Hoban suggests, no matter how powerful, is unlikely to change behavior patterns of a lifetime.

What are the rules and conventions of the kind of novel you're writing?

Are there certain expectations a reader is likely to have that your novel frustrates? What? What is your goal in breaking the rules?

"People who are more interested in form than in content play 'literary games.' I'm really only interested in life and how it should be lived. I see literature as part of that."—*Margaret Drabble*

A Writer's Journal

A writer's journal often includes more generally reflective, less completely personal kinds of entries than a diary. You might keep a record of how your novel is progressing and write your thoughts on what's pleasing or troubling you about it. You might also include scraps of overheard conversation, ideas you're worried you might not remember, exercises like the ones in this book, free-associative memories, passages copied from novels, responses to your reading. You don't have to keep your journal in a notebook; you can write on file cards and stick them in an envelope or a box, or store your notes in a computer file.

Keep a writer's journal, making at least an entry a day for a month. As an exercise, try to avoid straightforward diary-type entries ("As I had anticipated, Tuesday proved to be one of the worst days of my life"). After a month, include a couple of your favorites here.

"I collect envelopes of bits scribbled in inspiration on the bus, bits I wake up thinking about, and then have to find out what they mean and weave them in." —*Diane Johnson*

Scheduling

As you move into a more active novel-writing mode, you may need to change the way you spend some of your time. If your goal is to find an hour or two to write every day, start now by analyzing the way you currently schedule your time. Account briefly for every hour you spend over the course of the next week.

	MONDAY	TUESDAY	WEDNESDAY	THURSDAY
6-7				
7-8				
8-9				
9-10				
10-11				
11-12				
12-1				
1-2				
2-3				
3-4				
4-5				
5-6				
6-7				
7-8				
8-9				
9-10				
10-11				
11-12				
12-1				
1-2				
2-3				
3-4				
4-5				
5-6				

At the end of the week, go over your chart and note places where you could carve out more writing time. Then, for the next two weeks, find a block at least two hours long every single day to spend with your work. Stay up late, get up early, cut out inessentials (or essentials)—it's up to you. But make a commitment, for at least two weeks, to work every day, no excuses.

	FRIDAY	SATURDAY	SUNDAY
6-7			
7-8			
8-9			
9-10			
10-11			
11-12			
12-1			
1-2			
2-3			
3-4			
4-5			
5-6			
6-7			
7-8			
8-9			
9-10			
10-11			
11-12			
12-1			
1-2			
2-3			
3-4			
4-5			
5-6			

Flannery O'Connor worked in her study for four hours every morning and never regretted the time, even when no ideas came to her. "I go in every day, because if any idea comes between eight and noon, I'm there all set for it."

A Regular Routine

Sometimes it's impossible to stick to a routine, but it's often a good idea to try. Setting aside other activities can help you make writing the high priority in your life it deserves to be. A poet may be able to wait for the muse to visit, but a novelist usually must work hard, and often, to finish a book. French writer Jules Renard notes that the greatest writers are those who "toil eighteen hours a day without tiring." He continues, "Talent is a question of quantity. Talent does not write one page: it writes three hundred. . . . They exhaust the ink, they use up the paper. This is the only difference between men of talent and cowards who will never make a start."

After you've finished the exercise on pages 10–11 ("Scheduling"), think about the experience and answer the questions below.

At what time of day did I write?

Was this a good time? Would I work better at a different time? When? Why?

Was I faithful to my promise to write for a certain amount of time each day, or did I cheat?

On which day(s) did I do my best work? Why?

On which day(s) did I work least effectively? Why?

Considering the answers to these questions, set a new schedule for yourself and plan to follow it more or less (with an emphasis on more) faithfully until your work is finished. Write a few sentences describing the new schedule.

"In writing, habit seems to be a much stronger force than either willpower or inspiration. Consequently, there must be some little quality of fierceness until the habit pattern of a certain number of words is established. There is no possibility of saying, 'I'll do it if I feel like it.' " —*John Steinbeck*

Forces Beyond Your Control

Write about what is keeping you from completing (or beginning) your novel. Is it time? Money? Noisy living space? Inability to type? Writer's block? Worry that you're wasting your time? Uncertainty about what should happen next? Fear of ridicule?

Then, for each item, list all the ways you can think of to overcome that obstacle.

Most writers do have obstacles to overcome. As Rebecca West remarked in an interview, "I couldn't control the two wars!" Indeed, during the Second World War, West's writing time was disrupted by her responsibility for a large herd of cows. Often, the difference between a happy writer and a dissatisfied one is her relative success at getting past these obstacles. Sometimes, of course, things other than writing are going to have to take precedence. "At one time I had to write articles because I had to put up a lot of money for family reasons," West observes. "Everyone has to pay for their families now and then." But make sure your hiatus from writing is only temporary.

OBSTACLE   **WAYS TO OVERCOME IT**

"The only certainty about writing and trying to be a writer is that it has to be done, not dreamed of or planned and never written, or talked about (the ego eventually falls apart like a soaked sponge) but simply written; it's a dreadful, awful fact that writing is like any other work." —*Janet Frame*

The Central Problem

One way of beginning a novel is to start with a central social problem, moral dilemma, or abstract intellectual question that interests you. Robin Cook, writer of medical thrillers, including *Coma*, plans his novels by first conceiving a central problem that will affect the characters. In *Toxin*, the problem is the emergence of *E. coli* bacteria due to unsanitary slaughterhouse conditions. Cook then dramatizes this problem, imagining the death of the daughter of a powerful doctor from the bacteria and the doctor's efforts to avenge that death.

List problems or questions you might want to write about. Homelessness? Are there circumstances under which marital infidelity is acceptable? Who killed the president of Sweden? Why not build a bridge across the Bering Strait? List anything you can think of. Then explore why each problem interests you.

PROBLEM   **WHY DOES THIS SPARK YOUR INTEREST?**

Now choose one of the problems you listed above and imagine characters forced to deal with it. How will your characters be affected by your problem? How will they change physically, spiritually, or materially through their confrontation with it? What solution to the problem can you devise?

"Never present ideas except in terms of temperaments and characters." —*André Gide*

A Really Bad Book

On the lines below, write the title and author of the book you've read that you dislike more than any other. Spend some time thinking about this. You might want to list others you've disliked and then narrow it. Try to think of a book you dislike for reasons other than simply its genre. If you hate historical romances, for example, don't just choose *The Hidden Hyacinth* as your all-time least favorite just because it is a historical romance.

_____, by _____

In a paragraph or so explain what makes this book so bad. Again, be thoughtful. "It's long and boring" isn't enough. What makes it boring? Why do some long books hold your interest while others don't? Is the problem with the characters? The plot? The basic belief system of the writer?

If you were in charge of rewriting, what would you do to make the book better? Are there specific problems you should be careful to avoid in your own novel?

In 1820, James Fenimore Cooper wrote his first novel, *Precaution*, on a dare, after complaining to his wife, "I could write better than that," about a particularly bad novel. Although this first effort did not do well, Cooper learned from his early failure and went on to write more than fifty novels—many well received and still influential—during the next thirty years.

Tools

Being as specific as possible, list three to six of the tools you use for your writing. Note cards (like Anne Tyler, who writes, "When I make a note of new ideas on index cards, I imagine I'm clearing out my head")? First draft in red pencil on a yellow legal pad? Second draft with a fountain pen in a notebook with really tiny blue lines? Manual or electric typewriter? Tape recorder? Desktop computer or IBM ThinkPad? WordPerfect or Microsoft Works?

——————————————   ——————————————   ——————————————

——————————————   ——————————————   ——————————————

Ukrainian writer Irina Ratushinskaya, forbidden ordinary writing materials, wrote with sharpened matchsticks on soap while imprisoned for anti-Soviet agitation from 1983 to 1986. After memorizing her work, she washed her hands to conceal it from her guards. You don't have to do this. But consider whether the tools you're using are the most efficacious possible, given your personal habits, desires, and needs.

Write a few paragraphs with completely different tools than you've ever used for fiction writing.

Now think about the experience. If you'd like to write with something different from what you use now, why not switch? If your Rapidograph keeps leaking, buy a cleaning kit. If you can't afford a laptop computer, consider putting it on a credit card. If your response is, "But I can't do that!" ask yourself why not. Maybe it's time to start taking yourself more seriously as a writer, which could involve investing in a few good tools.

"The ideal view for daily writing, hour on hour, is the blank brick wall of a cold-storage warehouse. Failing this, a stretch of sky will do, cloudless if possible." —*Edna Ferber*

Beginning to Write

A Picture Outline

Here is Manuel Komroff's graphic chart showing the scenes, plot details, theme, pacing, time line, and some of the characters in his 1930 novel, *Coronet*, which recounts the shifting fortunes of the aristocratic de Senlis family over the course of about three hundred years. The chart is a kind of pictorial outline of the novel, a tiny replica of the novel showing every important issue Komroff planned to deal with as he began to write.

PLAN FOR CORONET

PART	TIME	THEME ARISTOCRACIES	COUNTRIES	HISTORIC FIGURES	PATH OF NOBILITY	PATH OF CORONET	THE TEN CRIMES	TEMPO and VIEWPOINT
I	Rennaissance 1600	The birth and glorification	Florence, Italy	none	A steady decline of nobility of character	Creation in shop of silversmith Rocco	The crimes grow in strength ... Theft	Slow No comments
II	Napoleonic 1812	The failure of military nobility (empire)	France in Russia	Napoleon	The blue blood of valor and its rewards	Dug out of tomb. Emiel. Sold to blacksmith Jeweler	...Drunkenness ...Greed ...Deception	Moderate
III	After Napoleon	The decline of aristocracy in civil life (lord and master)	Russia in France	none	The sons of a tailor vs. the old Count of Senlis	Coronet bought by new nobility ...	Snobbery	More Rapid A sly remark or two
IV	1849	The decline in the arts (patronage)	France	Chopin and Balzac	The nobles lose privilege	The Two sons of Count Burin...	Debauchery Jealousy	Fast
V	1900	The false aristocracy of intellect (superman)	The intellectual movements, mainly in Germany	Nietzsche	The intellectuals attempt to wear the crown	? ... ? ...	Arson Murder	Slow and reflective but
VI	1917-29	The aristocracy of money	Chicago, Paris	none	The titles thrive best under protection of money. America the happy hunting ground	? ...	Rape	Faster at finish

Create a graphic chart on the next page using column heads relevant to your own work. If your theme doesn't involve aristocracies, you don't need to worry about those. If Leo Tolstoy had created a chart for *The Death of Ivan Ilych*, for example, he might have devised a column devoted to incidents showing Ivan Ilych's moral decline—his marriage of convenience, his decision to change careers based only on salary, the obsession with interior decoration that leads to his fatal injury. To create your own chart, you will, however, need to think about what themes your novel *does* deal with. (See page 59 for more discussion of theme.) You'll also need to have a clear sense of its final shape, including its climax and conclusion.

If, after you've finished your chart, you find yourself with leftover scenes that don't seem to belong anywhere, ask yourself if you really need those scenes.

Here's what Komroff, the author of thirteen novels and a former Columbia University professor, has to say about his graphic chart: "During the long time that it takes to write a novel, many ideas will come to the mind of the novelist. A single glance at his graphic chart will inform him if his new idea is really part of his grand scheme or not. If it fits, he will see exactly the place where it may be included. If it does not fit, then the chart will have no room for it and thus assure the novelist that it is truly out of place. . . . If, however, the novelist, during the writing of his story, finds that some new material must absolutely be included, then he will have to stop work and starting from the very beginning reorganize and rebuild the entire structure of his novel. This reorganization will call for an entirely new graphic chart."

Writing Without an Outline

Even if you have no desire to make a strict outline of your plot before you begin, you probably already have *some* idea of what's going to happen. Make a rough list, in any order, of elements you know must appear. These can be characters, plot events, specific images—even if there's a lot you still haven't decided on. Ideally, this list can lead to more discoveries, helping you reach decisions on other elements you need to include but haven't decided on yet.

Jessica Hagedorn, for example, did not really have an idea of what she wanted to do when she began *Dogeaters*, but she did know "it was going to open in a movie theater. I knew it was going to be from this young girl's point of view. I knew that sometimes the character of Rio, the young girl, would speak in the first person and sometimes she wouldn't."

Mystery writer Patricia Cornwell says, "In *Postmortem* I wanted to use serial rape strangulations. And I wanted one of the victims to be a woman physician because I knew the projection that was going to go on with Scarpetta [her protagonist, a medical examiner], that that was going to be hard for her."

"There are two ways a novel can come together for anybody. One is answering to a plan. I've found over the years that doesn't work very well for me. I'll outline everything and then the outline becomes irrelevant. The writing I like the best is when I don't know what I'm doing. This is another way of saying, if I can foresee the shape of a book and if I can foresee the outcome of things I've set in motion, then that is almost a guarantee of its being too limited. I would rather be a sort of privileged reader in that I get to write what I get to read, and chance having to write six or seven hundred pages to produce a two-hundred-page book. Then there is an element of real, deep-down excitement about the process. It is the harder way to write a book, the wilder way." — *Thomas McGuane*

Names

Especially if you haven't named everyone in your novel yet, but even if you have, use this space to write some possibilities. It's important to remember the connotations of names, especially if you're using the characters' names to reflect their personalities. Margaret Mitchell first thought of calling Scarlett O'Hara of *Gone With the Wind* Pansy O'Hara, a name that seems far less appropriate than Scarlett to the character's intense, fiery personality.

Phone books can offer inspiration, as can colors, places on the map, historical figures, and baby name books. John Irving named Jennie Fields, the mother of Garp in *The World According to Garp*, after a fiction-writer classmate. J.D. Salinger's Holden Caulfield in *The Catcher in the Rye* was named for two actors, William Holden and Joan Caulfield.

In his "Book of Memoranda," Charles Dickens kept a list of possible names for characters, names he invented and names he found, for example, on a list of students attending a Privy Council school for poor children. Note that Dickens ended up using a few names from this list in novels, including *Doctor Marigold*, *Holiday Romance*, and *George Silverman's Explanation*.

Robert Ladle	Sarah Goldsacks	Joey Stick	Rosetta Dust	Bill Marigold
Susan Goldring	Stephen Marquick	Catherine Two	Henry Ghost	Matilda Rainbird
George Muzzle	Miriam Denial	Walter Ashes	Sophia Doomsday	Zephaniah Fury
Alice Thorneywork	William Why	Sally Gimblet	Robert Gospel	Verity Hawkyard
Thomas Fatherly	Birdie Nash	Robin Scubbam	Ambrosina Events	

Exploratory Research

The facts in your novel must be accurate so readers will believe in the scene you set. Spend at least two hours at the library, on the Internet, or with an expert, investigating an issue about which you now know little. Draw at least one diagram that will help you explain your research to your readers. List and define at least five unfamiliar vocabulary words that will help your character or scene appear authentic.

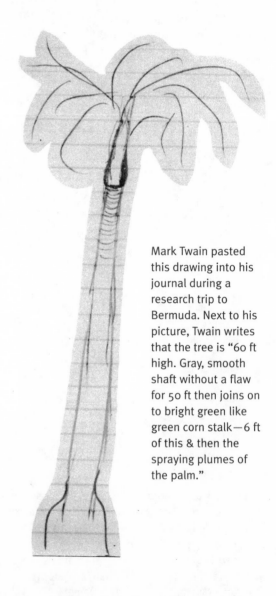

Mark Twain pasted this drawing into his journal during a research trip to Bermuda. Next to his picture, Twain writes that the tree is "60 ft high. Gray, smooth shaft without a flaw for 50 ft then joins on to bright green like green corn stalk—6 ft of this & then the spraying plumes of the palm."

"There is only one trick that marks the writer. He is always watching. It's a kind of trick of the mind and he is born with it." —*Morley Callaghan*

Hard Research

As opposed to going somewhere and soaking up atmosphere for your novel in a general way, think now of some specific piece of information you need to know, about a subject not completely unfamiliar to you, and do the necessary research. Detail the results of your research, and report any surprises.

Mystery novelist Sue Grafton, for example, visited a morgue specifically to investigate the latching mechanisms inside the drawers where the bodies are kept, having planned for a character to find herself in one. Would it be possible, she wondered, for her character to escape? "When I did the research," Grafton says, "what I discovered was that there are very few drawers. The drawers that you see in morgues in films and television shows are largely a fabrication of television writers."

"In *The Black Tower*, I have two of my characters climb cliffs in Dorset. I did want to get this right and use the right technical words and I wanted them to make a particular climb, a *known* climb, on a known cliff. And, as my son-in-law is a climber, he was kind enough to give me some details and I thought I would get this right. I settled down and I described this climb in great detail with two suspects [making the climb] and I wrote at the end, 'Ten minutes later, they flung themselves breathless on the grass on the top of the cliff.' When Peter came for the weekend with my daughter I said, 'Will you cast your eye over this and see if I've got it right?' And he gave a rich round of laughter and he said, 'My God, Mother-in-law, they certainly would have been breathless; they've done an eight-hour climb in ten minutes.' " —*P. D. James*

Am I Being Too Personal?

If your novel is autobiographical, think of the person you're writing about who would most likely be offended (or sue)—and change her beyond recognition. Write a scene in which this new character, with a new name, is introduced.

Are there reasons for keeping friends and family out of your novel? Perhaps. Writers, including Thomas Wolfe (*Look Homeward, Angel*), Grace Metalious (*Peyton Place*), and Truman Capote (*Answered Prayers*) have been dismayed by touchy reactions from real-life versions of fictional characters. Robert Tine, author of *State of Grace*, won a suit brought by his ex-girlfriend, who claimed readers recognized her in his protagonist, a high-class prostitute, because, like the character, Tine's ex-girlfriend spoke French fluently, had a degree in psychology, lived on Fourteenth Street in Manhattan, and had visited the Bahamas with an Iranian businessman. Terry McMillan won a suit brought by an ex-boyfriend, a construction worker, after publication of her *Disappearing Acts*, which portrays a difficult relationship between a songwriter and an uneducated construction worker. Other suits, however, have been settled in the plaintiff's favor. Much depends on the makeup of the individual jury.

In 1983, an interviewer asked Salman Rushdie about his novel *Shame*, which is critical of Pakistani political events and leaders: "Is there any danger to your family from the fact that you've written it?" Rushdie replied, "Not as far as I can see. It's only a novel, after all, written in the English language—which most people can't read—and it will be stopped from entering the country. I now have a British passport, so in that sense they can refuse me entry to the country or they can deport me if I get through, but that's about it—given that I haven't broken any law in Pakistan." Six years later, after the publication of *The Satanic Verses*, the Ayatollah Khomeini pronounced a *fatwa*, or death sentence, against Rushdie.

Varieties of Diction

A character's regional, ethnic, educational, and socioeconomic background will to some extent determine the kind of vocabulary he uses. Personality and interests also have a lot to do with dictating a character's speech patterns. Everyone talks a little differently, and much of what the reader learns comes through the characters' dialogue. Ideally, in a conversation with four characters, the reader will be able to figure out who said what, even without "he said" tag lines.

Nancy Mitford's 1956 *Noblesse Oblige* offers examples of specific words she found to be used either by upper-class or lower-class speakers.

UPPER-CLASS (U) USAGE	LOWER-CLASS (NON-U) USAGE
sick	ill
house	home
lavatory paper	toilet paper
knave (in cards)	jack
looking-glass	mirror

List of five or six of your main characters and for each list at least five words or phrases that only that character would use. One might swear a lot, for example; another might use outdated slang expressions; another might punctuate his sentences with a lot of "you know's" and "uh's"; another might use poetic metaphor; another might constantly bring in technical submarine-repair-related language.

"I wanted the book to feel a little bit like a chick sitting around gabbing, so when I was writing it, I'd go to open mikes and read sections. It does have a rhythm to it, but it's definitely written for the page, unlike some of my earlier stuff, which was written just for performance. It's as close to merging the two styles as I think you can get. When I read at book signings, though, I still edit it for performance, skipping over stuff when I know it'll move quicker for an audience." —*Maggie Estep*

Style

Choose a novel you admire and copy a favorite paragraph, one that demonstrates the writer's characteristic style.

Some writers strive to make their styles unobtrusive; other writers' styles are immediately recognizable. In *Exercises in Style*, Raymond Queneau tells an anecdote about a man who boards a bus and accuses another passenger of jostling him. Later, outside the train station, one of the bus rider's friends points out that he is missing a button on his coat. Queneau rewrites this simple story ninety-nine times, in ninety-nine separate styles, including a style rich with metaphors, one in which the story is told backward, one using the imagery of a dream, and in styles featuring the present tense, the passive voice, and the language of poetry and drama.

While, to a degree, your style must come to you naturally, you can be aware of stylistic elements that are particularly effective (think of Ernest Hemingway's deceptively simple sentences, for example, with their hypnotic repetitions) or ineffective (too much passive voice, lack of variety in sentence construction).

Rewrite the paragraph in the style of another writer you admire. If you've copied a paragraph from *A Farewell to Arms*, for example, rewrite it in the style of William Faulkner, with his long, ruminative sentences.

Rewrite the paragraph again using your personal writing style.

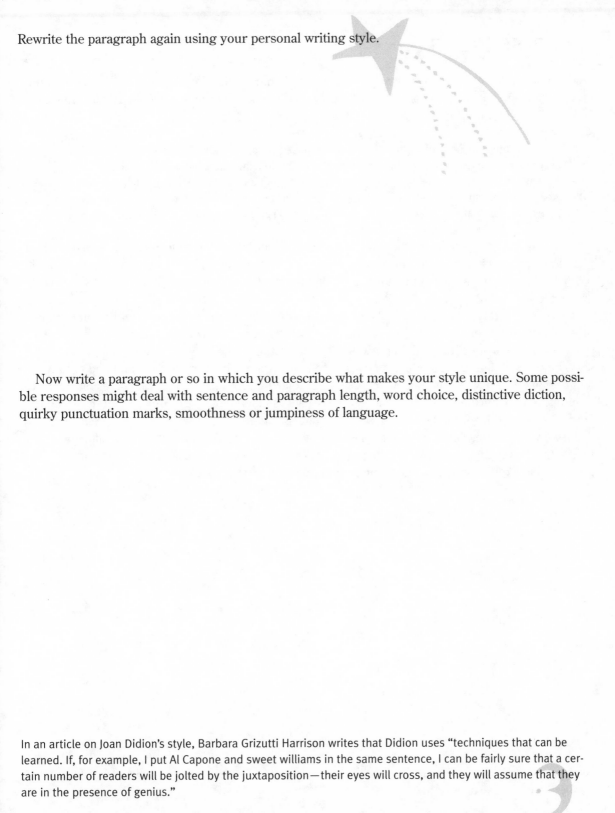

Now write a paragraph or so in which you describe what makes your style unique. Some possible responses might deal with sentence and paragraph length, word choice, distinctive diction, quirky punctuation marks, smoothness or jumpiness of language.

In an article on Joan Didion's style, Barbara Grizutti Harrison writes that Didion uses "techniques that can be learned. If, for example, I put Al Capone and sweet williams in the same sentence, I can be fairly sure that a certain number of readers will be jolted by the juxtaposition—their eyes will cross, and they will assume that they are in the presence of genius."

Perverse Plans

Ask yourself if you are putting obstacles in the way of your reader. Perhaps you are using difficult, off-putting language. The final section of James Joyce's *Ulysses* begins with Molly Bloom lying in bed, musing about her life.

> Yes because he never did a thing like that before as ask to get his breakfast in bed with a couple of eggs since the *City Arms* hotel when he used to be pretending to be laid up with a sick voice doing his highness to make himself interesting to that old faggot Mrs Riordan that he thought he had a great leg of and she never left us a farthing all for masses for herself and her soul greatest miser ever was actually afraid to lay out 4d for her methylated spirit telling me all her ailments

This may not be a problem. Works by other writers including Gertrude Stein, Thomas Pynchon, John Barth, and Don DeLillo do find enthusiastic and respectful readers. But if you are a "difficult" writer, you should be aware of it, and be sure that the obstacles you place in the way of the reader are deliberate and necessary.

There are obstacles other than difficult language that you might be creating, either on purpose or inadvertently. Thomas McGuane, for example, remembers, "I was once going to write a detective novel in the form of a cookbook. I was hell-bent just to shake up the kaleidoscope." Now, he says, however, "I find it hard enough to write well, giving myself all the tools I can handle. I no longer think it necessary to make it crazy or write a six-hundred-page novel that takes place in two minutes." Other hurdles to finding and keeping readers include obscure subject matter, extreme length, unusual (or no) paragraphing, and phonetic spelling.

List any difficulties you're creating for your reader, from myriad—and possibly confusing—plot twists, to unsympathetic characters, to graphic sex and violence, to demanding forms and language. Then explain why these challenges are necessary to your book.

"If you write a story of ten thousand pages, no matter whether it is good or not, no one is going to publish it and no one is going to read it." —*Isaac Bashevis Singer*

Listening to Storytellers

Retell a memorable story someone has told you, being as faithful as possible to the voice of the teller. Indeed, for this exercise, the voice of the storyteller should be every bit as important as the story being told. What does the story say about the storyteller? Does the teller relate the story in a straightforward way, or are there digressions? Does he interrupt himself? What prompted the storyteller to start talking?

Remember that the oral tradition is alive in novels: Some contain storyteller characters; others are narrated by someone apparently speaking aloud. The events in Fannie Flagg's *Fried Green Tomatoes at the Whistle Stop Café* are told in part by Dot Weems in *The Weems Weekly,* a newspaper that owes more to the oral tradition than to the written one.

> Idgie says that she has a genuine shrunken head from headhunters in South America, and it is on the counter at the café if you want to see it.
>
> Is there anybody out there that can cure snoring? If so, come over to my house. My other half is about to drive me insane. I might send him out to the dogs. Even one of his old hounds snores, just like he does. I told him the other day, it must run in the family. Ha ha.

Is there anything in the story you've recounted that you can use in your novel? Are there other stories you've been told that you might want to work into the book? What makes the story you heard so memorable?

"My mother and my mother's mother and my mother's sisters were wonderful storytellers but there are no real-life counterparts to any of my characters. Graham Greene said that all good novelists have bad memories. What you remember comes out as journalism; what you forget goes into the compost of the imagination."

—*Robert Olen Butler*

Evenly Matched Characters

Your protagonist will almost certainly need a worthy opponent. If your main character is smarter, nicer, richer, *and* harder working than the other characters, your reader's interest may falter, because it's likely that the protagonist will eventually prosper.

That's not to say that your protagonist and your antagonist have to be identical in their strengths, however. Paul Pennyfeather, the young divinity student in Evelyn Waugh's *Decline and Fall*, is far smarter and kinder than his greedy guardian and amoral fiancée, but his credulous nature and poverty make his power about equal to theirs, and it's no surprise when he ends up unjustly imprisoned.

In each of the categories below, give your protagonist and antagonist a numerical value, with 10 being high and 0 low.

	PROTAGONIST	ANTAGONIST
Intelligence	_____	_____
Personality traits	_____	_____
Good looks	_____	_____
Health	_____	_____
Career success	_____	_____
Wealth	_____	_____
Power and status	_____	_____
Diligence and industry	_____	_____
Lucky breaks	_____	_____
Moral uprightness	_____	_____
Support from other characters	_____	_____
Other_____	_____	_____

If you'd like, assign a weight to the different categories, or omit some altogether if they seem irrelevant. Add other categories depending on the circumstances of your novel.

After you've added your scores, if your protagonist has over ten points more than your antagonist, consider adding a few positive qualities to your antagonist or taking a few from your hero. Don't worry, though, if your protagonist has fewer points than your antagonist, even many fewer points; think, for example, of the satisfying success of Chance, the innocent, slow-witted, but incredibly decent and lucky hero of Jerzy Kosinski's *Being There*.

"If you are inclined to leave your character solitary for any considerable length of time, better question yourself. Fiction is association, not withdrawal." —*A.B. Guthrie, Jr.*

Auditioning Characters

Think about a place in your novel where you know you're going to need to introduce a new character. This can be early, when the main characters first appear, or later, after the basic situation has been established. Then consider the options you have in the creation of this new person. For example, suppose things have been going badly enough for your protagonist, and you know that the arrival of her brother-in-law is going to make things even worse. But worse in what way? Unlike in life, you have a lot of leeway in creating the brother-in-law's specific variety of badness. Will he try to get custody of the character's children? Control her finances? Are his experiments with rodent brains even more ominous than they initially appear?

Briefly note the plot circumstances that demand a new character, one whose personality traits you have not yet established.

Now write a paragraph introducing your new character. What does he look like? Act like? After you're finished, consider rewriting the paragraph introducing a different new character. Remember that, unlike a real casting director, you have a virtually unlimited number of audition candidates to choose from.

Talking about why he chose Richard Nixon as the main narrator of *The Public Burning*, Robert Coover says, "I wanted someone who lived inside the mythology, accepting it, and close to the center, yet not quite the center, off to the edge a bit, an observer. A number of characters auditioned for the part, but Nixon, when he appeared, proved ideal."

Know the End at the Beginning

Even if you're not sure yet of the events that will occur in the middle pages, you might find it helpful to know right away how you're going to end it. This knowledge will help you work with fore-shadowing and symbols as you progress through your book, and may help you avoid writing scenes that you'll have to cut later because they don't fit with your ending.

Here's an exercise to do as soon as possible after you've begun (or even before you've put words on paper). Spend some time revising and polishing a passage that could become the final paragraph, and write what you now see as your final version. When you're finished, note the date so you won't forget.

date: _____

After you've been working for a few months, cover up the final paragraph you wrote previously, and, once again, write what you see as the concluding sentences of your novel.

date: _____

Compare your two final paragraphs. Has there been much change? If the changes are only cosmetic, is this because you are pleased with your original perception of the conclusion? If so, congratulations! If you're not happy with the results of your writing of the final paragraph, ask yourself why not. Are there aspects of your plot that you're still not sure about?

Make a list or write a couple of paragraphs regarding any questions you still need to answer about your plot. For example, you know that the climax will be two of your characters' discovery of something truly horrifying on a walk in a secluded stretch of woods—something meant to shock the reader as well as the characters. But what?

"When I start I have a pretty well developed idea what the book is about and how it ought to go, because generally I've been thinking about it and making notes for months if not years. Generally I have the ending in mind, usually the last paragraph almost verbatim. I begin at the beginning and stay close to the track, if it's a track and not a whalepath. If it turns out I'm in the open sea, my compass is my narrative instinct, with an assist by that astrolabe, theme. The destination, wherever it is, is, as I said, already defined. If I go astray it's not a long excursus, good for getting to know the ocean if not the world. The original idea, altered but recognizable, on the whole remains."—*Bernard Malamud*

Living Right

Unless, like Ernest Hemingway, Thomas Wolfe, and Victor Hugo, you write standing up (and even then, really), you may not be getting the exercise you need. Or maybe your writing regime has led you to other habits some would consider bad (overeating, sleep deprivation, neglect of other obligations). Getting up at five to write for two hours before work may be making you cranky. Staying up until two to write may be hurting your marriage.

Describe whatever bad habits or other behavior you feel writing has led you to (as opposed to bad habits you had before you started your novel).

Now list what you can do to improve your life during the coming months or years as you complete your novel. This plan, of course, will be different for every writer. Kate Braverman, for example, whose students call her system "Braverman's Boot Camp," calls for no TV watching, reading aloud two hours a day, long walks alone in the hills, and always carrying a notebook. Your own plan may call for no time spent reading aloud, for example, and five twenty-minute writing sessions every day.

"I just feel my job is to keep myself healthy and alert and physically fit for the task of writing, which is very hard physical labor. . . .So I probably exercise two hours a day altogether, otherwise I don't know how to offset the tension and the stress of just inertia." —*Sue Grafton*

Necessities

Titles

The title is your first chance to create your novel's own particular brand of magic—and to grab your reader's attention. Here are some sources of title inspiration that writers in the past and present have found fruitful; you'll notice that some titles fall naturally into more than one category. Because your first idea for a title may not be your best, even if you have already thought of a title for your novel, create a new one based on each of the formulas below.

SOURCE	TITLE	YOUR TITLE
The Bible	*Exodus* Leon Uris	_____
Shakespeare	*The Sound and the Fury* William Faulkner	_____
Popular Culture	*Waiting for the End of the World* Madison Smartt Bell	_____
Theme	*Crime and Punishment* Fyodor Dostoyevsky	_____
Subject	*A Passage to India* E.M. Forster	_____
Character's Name	*Debby* Max Steele	_____
Central Image	*The Scarlet Letter* Nathaniel Hawthorne	_____
Catchphrase from Novel	*Up the Down Staircase* Bel Kaufman	_____
Setting	*Bullet Park* John Cheever	_____
Alliteration	*Pride and Prejudice* Jane Austen	_____
Time Reference	*Never Come Morning* Nelson Algren	_____

F. Scott Fitzgerald kept a list of titles that appealed to him, both promising ones and really awful ones, even when he didn't have a particular story in mind to go with the title. Here are some of his ideas. • Journal of a Pointless Life • Tall Women • Wore Out His Welcome • Birds in the Bush • "Your Cake" • Napoleon's Coat • Jack a Dull Boy • Tavern Music, Boat Trains • Dark Circles • Police at the Funeral • The Parvenu Hat • The Bed in the Ball Room

Motivation

Most of your characters will have definite reasons for what they do. Some reasons will be more admirable than others, of course, and some will be misinterpreted by other characters—but it's best if they're not misinterpreted by the reader. You must establish sufficient motivation. Unless you mean for your character to be perceived as psychotic, you will probably not have her plan to kill her husband just because he doesn't put the lid on the trash can.

List your main characters, their primary goals, and the main motivating factors governing their actions. If you show your writing to other people, this might be a particularly interesting page to show them to see if they have the same perception of your characters' motivations as you do. The example comes from Dorothy West's *The Wedding*:

CHARACTER	IMMEDIATE GOAL	ULTIMATE MOTIVATION
Lute	Stop Shelby's marriage	Penetration of Ovalite high society
Shelby	Meet with Lute	Curiosity, lust, guilt over impending marriage to white man
Della	Visit Lute on island	Misguided love, desire to reunite with husband and daughter

Talking about the characters in his books, novelist Robert Stone says, "Always in these novels people are trying to get out of the box they're in. As in life, they don't often succeed very well. But they are always catching glimmers of something outside themselves that may be able to save them."

Opening Sentences

In the same way that you considered various title possibilities before making a final decision, you don't want to settle, necessarily, for the first opening sentence that comes to mind. After each example, write an opening for your novel according to the following categories.

Character as a Child: "As a child, on the Red River plantation where he was born, Little Augie was not required to chop cotton or work in the rice swamp like the other boys of his age. He was considered too frail for hard labor. Instead it became his duty to mind the cows when they grazed in the clover fields and to lead the horses to the watering-place" (Arna Bontemps, *God Sends Sunday*).

Physical Description of Character: ""He was thick-chested and light-haired, with sloping shoulders joined so smoothly to his neck he seemed not to have any neck at all, and a head whose size made his shoulders look narrower than they were, a wide round head which he cocked slightly forward when he walked, swinging his arms as if he meant to smash through whatever stood in his way" (Philip Caputo, *Horn of Africa*).

Place: "On the pleasant shore of the French Riviera, about half way between Marseilles and the Italian border, stands a large, proud, rose-colored hotel. Deferential palms cool its flushed façade, and before it stretches a short dazzling beach. Lately it has become a summer resort of notable and fashionable people; a decade ago it was almost deserted after its English clientele went north in April" (F. Scott Fitzgerald, *Tender is the Night*).

Weather: "It was a cold grey day in late November. The weather had changed overnight, when a backing wind brought a granite sky and a mizzling rain with it, and although it was now only a little after two o'clock, in the afternoon the pallour of a winter evening seemed to have closed upon the hills, cloaking them in mist. It would be dark by four" (Daphne du Maurier, *Jamaica Inn*).

Dream: "One morning in late March, a Friday, Freddy Landon awaked from a dream about his daughter. It was a weird dream in which he watched helplessly while his daughter and a young man named Ralph Chamberlain set fire to his apartment building. They were both naked as babes and they laughed wildly as he roasted in the flames" (Richard B. Wright, *In the Middle of a Life*).

Statement of Philosophy: "I don't know about Will Rogers, but I grew up deciding the world was nothing but a sad, dangerous junk pile heaped with shabby geegaws, the bullies who peddled them, and the broken-up human beings who worked the line" (Michael Malone, *Time's Witness*).

Travel: "On a winter evening of the year 19—, after arduous travels across two continents and as many centuries, pursued by harsh weather and threatened with worse, an aging emeritus professor from an American university, burdened with illness, jet lag, great misgivings, and an excess of luggages, eases himself and his encumbrances down from his carriage onto a railway platform in what many hold to be the most magical city in the world, experiencing not so much that hot terror which initiates are said to suffer when their eyes first light on an image of eternal beauty, as rather that cold chill that strikes lonely travelers who find themselves in the wrong place at the wrong time" (Robert Coover, *Pinocchio in Venice*).

Death: "Standing amid the tan, excited post-Christmas crowd at the Southwest Florida Regional Airport, Rabbit Angstrom has a funny sudden feeling that what he has come to meet, what's floating in unseen about to land, is not his son Nelson and daughter-in-law Pru and their children but something more ominous and intimately his: his own death, shaped vaguely like an airplane" (John Updike, *Rabbit at Rest*).

"I very much enjoy writing novels, but the beginning of a novel is a time of awful torment, when you're dealing with a lot of dead pieces and you have to wait and wait for some kind of animation." —*Iris Murdoch*

Dialogue and Exposition

Use conversation between two or more characters to reveal something about the basic dramatic situation of your novel.

To be effective, dialogue will usually serve more than a single purpose. It can reveal character (and the characters' skill at conversation), allow the writer a chance to ponder important issues by letting characters discuss them, move the plot forward, and let relationships develop and deteriorate. You can also use dialogue to reveal the novel's basic dramatic situation if you do it cleverly (*not*, "Gee, Lily, isn't it lucky your violent but probably well-meaning husband, Paul, divorced Valerie, an unemployed kindergarten teacher, four years ago and that you bought this lovely Spanish-style home together—even if he did make you throw out your Kiss tapes?").

In the first paragraphs of Louisa May Alcott's *Little Women*, the basic situation of the four sisters' lives—their poverty, their love for their parents, their mildly discordant personalities—is revealed through dialogue.

> "Christmas won't be Christmas without any presents," grumbled Jo, lying on the rug.
>
> "It's so dreadful to be poor!" sighed Meg, looking down at her old dress.
>
> "I don't think it's fair for some girls to have plenty of pretty things, and other girls nothing at all," added little Amy, with an injured sniff.
>
> "We've got father and mother and each other," said Beth contentedly, from her corner.

"I try an exercise with a class I teach on fairy tales. . . . Sometimes I give a scene in which no dialogue takes place and the scene is done in a few sentences. I ask the class to put it into a dialogue. Hidden characters emerge; it's astonishing what happens when you take something that's told very abruptly, and suddenly you listen to it as speech." —*Nancy Willard*

Make a Good Character Look Bad

Create a scene in which your character does one of the following:
- is hurt or humiliated
- does something stupid
- makes a fool of herself
- knowingly commits an immoral act or does not speak up when someone else does
- shows through her speech or actions that she is wrong about something important

Some writers fall so much in love with their protagonists or identify so closely with them that the authors are unwilling to get these characters into any serious trouble. But a novel in which your character does nothing wrong will end up shorter than you had hoped. Even the generally sensitive, intelligent Lucy Honeychurch, in E.M. Forster's *A Room With a View,* convinces herself that she is in love with the snobbish, controlling Cecil Vyse and, early on, snubs several much more genuinely admirable characters. When she finally breaks up with Cecil, she does so awkwardly, in a scene that hardly shows her at her best.

Even if you haven't had terribly good luck marketing your short fiction, it's important not to despair of eventually getting your novel published. Discussing his decision to move from writing stories to writing novels, Pulitzer prize winner William Kennedy notes, "Having failed miserably as a short story writer, I decided it was time to go out and fail miserably as a novelist."

Memorable Minor Characters

Write a scene in which you make a minor character vivid through a single quirk or personality trait.

By now, your major characters are probably complex and distinct, each with a number of personality traits, and a full plate of past experiences that have made them what they are today. But you will likely have minor characters, too—characters with only a single, easily identifiable characteristic. These characters often need to be unique but not too complex.

Because Alfredo Santayana, in John Welter's *I Want to Buy a Vowel*, speaks little English, for example, it is difficult for the other characters to know much about him. Even the readers know what he's thinking only through his few English phrases: "I'm not going to pay a lot for this muffler," "My broker is E.F. Hutton," and "I want to buy a vowel." Alfredo's zany optimism about life in America is his only real personality trait, and it is expressed only through TV catchphrases. Even so, Santayana becomes a vivid and memorable character.

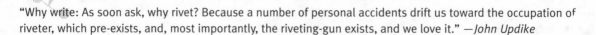

"Why write: As soon ask, why rivet? Because a number of personal accidents drift us toward the occupation of riveter, which pre-exists, and, most importantly, the riveting-gun exists, and we love it." —*John Updike*

Moving Your Characters Around

Think about passages in which characters must move from one place to another. Then write some sentences where you make those moves clear. For example, walk some characters from the kitchen to the backyard (and vice versa). Or write a few sentences where your character moves from a safe place to one where she will have to explain herself if she is discovered. Or write a brief transition from the car after a long, solitary drive to a party full of hostile strangers.

Most often, writers want their scene changes to be unobtrusive. Some novelists even divide their chapters like scenes in a play, with a new chapter beginning every time a change of scene is called for. That way writers can skip unexciting sentences, such as "She drove the station wagon to the bank."

On the other hand, stage directions can do more than move characters around; they can also help establish personalities or advance the plot. In John Barth's *The End of the Road*, a psychologist happens to notice that Jacob Horner has been sitting in the same position in the train depot for the last eleven hours. The doctor, who is black and not allowed in the depot's coffee shop, asks Horner to buy a couple of cups of coffee. Jacob Horner at this point has to move from the waiting area to the coffee shop, not a terribly exciting trip.

> "All right." I turned and walked with dignity toward the lounge, just off the concourse.
> "Fast!" the doctor laughed behind me. I flushed, and impulsively quickened my step.

Here, Barth takes advantage of the walk, making a point about the dynamics of the future relationship between the characters as well as simply emphasizing Jacob's slowness.

"Because one has written other books does not mean the next becomes any easier. Each book in fact is a tabula rasa; from book to book I seem to forget how to get characters in and out of rooms—a far more difficult task than the nonwriter might think." —*John Gregory Dunne*

Character Questionnaire

Answer these questions as if you were a character in your novel. You may even want to create a separate questionnaire for each important character. Note that some of your characters may be unlikely to fill out this kind of questionnaire truthfully; in this case, you must step in and answer honestly for the characters. Your goal is to get to know your characters well enough that you know how they're likely to respond to the situations in which they find themselves.

Name _____ Birthdate_____

Address _____House or apartment?_____

What kind of car do you drive? _____ Present profession _____

Annual salary _____Savings and other investments _____

What jobs have you had prior to your present one? _____

Marital status _____ Name, age, and profession of spouse/partner _____

_____

How satisfied are you with your present marriage or relationship?_____

Is your sex life adequate? _____

How did your last relationship end? _____

If you are not in a relationship, would you like to be?_____ With whom? _____

If you have children, what are their names and ages? _____

_____

What degrees have you completed? _____

From which schools? _____

Where were you born? _____ Where did you grow up _____

In general, was your childhood happy? _____ Why? _____

Your father's name and profession _____

Your mother's name and profession _____

Brothers' and sisters' names, ages, and professions _____

_____

What is your height? _____Weight? _____Hair color?_____Eye color? _____

Do you have any concerns about your health? _____

What medications do you use frequently? _____

What sports or other exercise do you participate in?_____

How much do you smoke tobacco or drink alcohol? _____

Do you abuse other drugs? What and how much? _____

Have you ever committed a crime or been arrested?_____

Do you tend to worry a lot? _____About what?_____

Have you ever seen a psychologist or psychiatrist? _____Why and for how long? _____

_____

Would you describe yourself as outgoing or diffident? _____

A leader or a follower? _____

Practical or a dreamer? _____

Who are your closest friends? _____

Do you have enemies? If so, who? _____

What conflicts among your friends or enemies concern you? _____

_____

What kind of music do you listen to? _____

Do you like to read? What? _____

Your favorite TV show and movie _____

Your most prized possession _____

Other hobbies or special interests _____

What political beliefs do you hold? _____

_____

Do you practice any religion? _____

What clubs or organizations do you belong to? _____

_____

Do you have any special artistic, musical or other talents? _____

What ambitions do you have that you have not yet fulfilled? _____

_____

What would you consider your greatest achievement to date? _____

"I know my characters. I know where they came from, who their grandmothers were, how their parents treated them with they were little." —Danielle Steel

The First Big Confliict

Write the scene in which the first big conflict appears.

With most novels, you know there's trouble ahead, but for a while—for a sentence or a paragraph or a chapter at the beginning of the book—everything seems to be going along just fine. Peter Benchley's *Jaws* begins as a young couple is about to go for a swim in the ocean but then instead make love "with urgent ardor on the cold sand." For a moment it seems they've avoided danger, but then the young woman goes in to swim after all, and "the fish sensed a change in the sea's rhythm."

Carol Anshaw's *Seven Moves* begins with psychologist Chris Snow experiencing normal daily difficulties: an aching back; a slightly obstinate client; her mildly aloof and distant girlfriend, Taylor; her gambler father's desire to borrow eleven hundred dollars. Any of these problems could easily intensify. On the other hand, Chris' backache could go away on its own; eleven hundred dollars is no more than Chris can afford. The first major conflict appears on page 29, when Chris finds a dinner guest "playfully biting the base of Taylor's thumb."

"Learning to write comes from your own recognition of what is wrong in your own work." —*Nadine Gordimer*

Subplot

You probably have an idea of what the main narrative line will be, and because you're writing a novel rather than a short story, you'll probably include subplots as well. List and briefly describe each of your subplots. Try to determine the thematic purpose of each one. Does it act as an echo, for example, or in counterpoint to your main plot?

In some novels, subplots will eventually form part of the main plot. In Peter Høeg's *Smilla's Sense of Snow*, the main plot involves Smilla's search for the murderer of her neighbor's son. A subplot involves Smilla's love affair with a man she meets during her investigation. Ultimately, it turns out that the man is more involved in the murder than she had originally realized; the two plots become one.

Of course, not all subplots inevitably join the main plot. In Ken Kesey's *One Flew Over the Cuckoo's Nest*, the main plot involves the struggle of Chief Bromden to regain his sanity after many years of institutionalization. There are subplots in the novel, mostly concerning the lives of other mental patients. One patient, Billy Bibbit, does not seem as disturbed as others but is eventually driven to suicide by the evil Big Nurse. The Billy Bibbit subplot is related thematically to the other plots, but Billy Bibbit's actual fate affects the characters psychologically rather than practically.

SUBPLOT #1

SUBPLOT #2

SUBPLOT #3

"Most writers enjoy only two brief periods of happiness. First when what seems a glorious idea comes flashing into mind and, secondly, when a last page has been written and you have not yet had time to consider how much better it all ought to have been." —J.B. Priestley

Multiple Plot Elements

Charlotte Brontë's *Jane Eyre* opens with a conflict between Jane and Mrs. Reed, who cruelly forces Jane to sleep in the room where Mrs. Reed's husband died. That conflict seems to end after four chapters, however, when Jane is sent away to school, where new difficulties arise. These difficulties, too, seem to end, though, when Jane leaves school to go to work for Mr. Rochester. But in chapter twenty-one, on her deathbed, Mrs. Reed calls for Jane for a final confrontation. Although other battles have emerged and superseded the original conflict, the Mrs. Reed story is never dropped entirely. Like most novelists, Brontë juggles several plotlines at once, bringing them to the forefront and letting them recede at different times over the course of the novel.

Here is a chart by Thomas H. Uzzell, a fiction editor at *Collier's*, showing the shape of a hypothetical novel, this one with seven plotlines that resolve and recur.

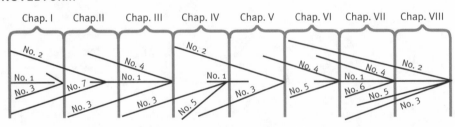

Patterns of short story and novel

In a diagram like the one above, show in which chapters you will dramatize each of the various plotlines of your novel.

"To me, [fiction is] revealing a pattern in the chaos, seeking for a pattern. There isn't necessarily a pattern. It's one's duty, it's one's nature to look for the pattern. But there may not be one. And if at the end of the day or at the end of the novel you see there is no pattern, or that it really is just bad luck for all the characters, then you have to face it." —*Margaret Drabble*

The Beginning of the Middle

Most novels begin with a number of questions. According to Don DeLillo, you know you've left the early, expository section behind and reached the middle when the first of the questions your novel raises is answered. Pinpoint the spot where your middle begins. How do you know? What is the first question to be answered?

In Richard Bausch's *Mr. Field's Daughter*, Annie, to her father's horror and regret, marries and becomes pregnant at nineteen. Questions arise: Is Annie's husband as bad as her father believes, or is he jealously overreacting? When Annie divorces her husband and later becomes engaged to another man, will the first husband care? On page 30, the answers begin: Annie's ex-husband, a drug addict, really is as bad as her father has feared, and it's clear that he's going to cause major problems for the family. With this information, the middle of the novel has begun.

"In the beginning I work brief shifts. The important mechanics are mental. A lot of mental testing goes on. Promising threads develop out of certain ideas or characters, and some of these lines reach almost to the end of the book, or out into infinity, since the book doesn't have anything resembling an end at this point. Other lines are very short. . . . Past the early stages I work longer periods. I find myself nearing the end of certain early lines of thought. This represents progress. It reminds me that the work doesn't actually go out into infinity. These identical, shapeless, satisfying days will come to an end somewhere down the line." —*Don DeLillo*

Second Crisis

While your novel will probably have only a single passage that can be described as a climax, it will likely have many crises—moments of high tension where incidents occur that significantly affect the characters' lives.

Maxine, in Bebe Moore Campbell's *Singing in the Comeback Choir*, seems to have her life pretty much in order: She's happily married, pregnant, and executive producer of a popular TV talk show. The first crisis occurs when it becomes clear that Maxine's beloved grandmother is no longer able to take care of herself, and Maxine must go from Los Angeles to Philadelphia to make arrangements for her grandmother's care.

The second crisis builds on the first. While in Philadelphia, Maxine talks by phone with members of her talk show team and realizes that her prestigious job is less secure than she had assumed. This second crisis raises new questions: Will Maxine leave her grandmother and return to Los Angeles? Even if she does, will she be able to save her job?

On page 46, you wrote about the first conflict in your novel. Here, in a few paragraphs, explain your second major crisis and how it will be resolved.

"Many times it's still a complete shock to me to just see a finished book and say, 'How did you ever manage to accomplish that?' But it's an accumulation of time. You spend every day doing it, and you spend enough days together in a row, then you've got a book. It's like building a house. It may be real hard—the days may be real hot or real cold when you're doing it—but after the house is finished, no matter how tired your muscles have been on all those other days, the memory of the work is something that goes away. You're left with the finished product." —*Larry Brown*

Lulls

Conflict and disorder may be a big part of your novel. Without them, you probably wouldn't have a novel. Still, even in the terrible lives of the most doomed characters, there will be moments when everything seems to be going pretty much as they had hoped, and dramatizing these moments adds richness and variety to your book.

In Jane Austen's *Sense and Sensibility*, seventeen-year-old Marianne meets dashing Mr. Willoughby early. They fall in love, showing clearly that their minds and hearts are completely attuned. If no further complications in their romance arose, if Marianne and Willoughby's delight in each other's company continued unabated, the plot would ultimately seem rather thin. Fortunately, however, Willoughby leaves Marianne abruptly, breaking her heart and leaving her miserable for many months to come. Still, the joyousness of their early love can never be completely forgotten.

Write about a happy moment in the life of one of your characters who is destined for trouble in the future.

"I write and write and write, and rewrite, and even if I retain only a single page from a full day's work, it *is* a single page, and these pages add up. As a result I have acquired the reputation over the years of being prolific when in fact I am measured against people who simply don't work as hard or as long." —*Joyce Carol Oates*

Scouting Locations

List all of the places where the action of your novel will occur. Include the locations even for scenes you haven't written yet and aren't sure you will. It might be useful to imagine your novel as if you were a filmmaker with an unlimited budget and in charge of scouting locations for the movie version.

_____   _____   _____

_____   _____   _____

_____   _____   _____

_____   _____   _____

_____   _____   _____

_____   _____   _____

_____   _____   _____

Decide whether you have included the right number of different places. There's no single answer for this. There are novels whose characters constantly move around and those in which there is hardly any physical motion. Almost all of Leonard Michaels' *The Men's Club* takes place in the house of one of the club members, as the men eat dinner and discuss their lives.

One way of judging whether you have the right amount is to consider the number of locations used in works you particularly admire. List all of the locations used in a novel of your choice. It is a good idea to have the novel in front of you as you write.

Title: _____

_____   _____   _____

_____   _____   _____

_____   _____   _____

_____   _____   _____

_____   _____   _____

Now look at the list of locations in your own novel. Are there more or fewer than on the second list? Underline the places on your list that excite you the most. Consider crossing out any that seem dull or that occur in scenes you dread writing.

If you're concerned that your list is too short, consider adding some new locations. This time, list at least fifteen places that interest you, whether or not they relate to your novel: the overgrown orchard at your old summer camp, the parking lot of a failing shopping mall, the dorm room of a strange college acquaintance.

_____   _____   _____

_____   _____   _____

_____   _____   _____

_____   _____   _____

_____   _____   _____

Are there locations from this list that should become part of your novel? Ask yourself if your description of place would become more sparkling if you moved everything from Honolulu to Chicago.

Pick the most exciting locations you can think of and, if possible, visit them. Photograph the houses, caves, or office buildings where your scenes are set. If visiting isn't an option, find magazine photos that reflect as closely as possible your exact locales. Now explain which locations, from any of your lists, are your favorites and why.

"When I was writing *Searches and Seizures*, I was living in London, and I needed to describe a hotel room. I've been in lots of hotel rooms, of course, but I didn't want to depend upon my memory. And so I went to the Royal Garden Hotel in Kensington and rented a room, simply to study the furniture there, to feel the glossy top of the wood that is almost not wood, to get the smell of the shower, the textures in the bath, to look at the rhetoric on the cards on top of the television set. This is stuff that I could not invent, and it was important to me to have it down very, very accurately. So I took notes. Somebody watching me would have thought I was a madman."

—*Stanley Elkin*

Third Crisis

On page 46, you explained the first crisis—a moment of high tension where events occur that will significantly affect the lives of one or more of your characters. On page 50, you described your second crisis.

The longer your novel, the more crises you're likely to have. Looking back to page 50, consider again the first two crises in Bebe Moore Campbell's *Singing in the Comeback Choir*. In a shorter novel, Maxine's grandmother and career problems could be enough. But here, a third crisis occurs, when Maxine phones her husband on a Saturday and he doesn't answer. She begins to wonder if he is being unfaithful to her, as he has been before. New questions are raised. Is Maxine's husband unfaithful? If not, will Maxine's groundless suspicions ruin their marriage?

Singing in the Comeback Choir is full of crises: children of Maxine's grandmother's friends face inner-city drug and pregnancy problems; Maxine's grandmother, given the opportunity to revive her singing career, finds it difficult to work with a new voice coach. Explain your third major crisis and how it will be resolved. Your novel may have many more than three crises. If so, you might create a separate page to describe each one.

"I try to get the right people assembled, give them right-sounding names, and then I'm off and running. The characters have to interact. Sometimes, when there's a confrontation, I don't know which way it's going to turn out—which character is going to come out of the house alive. Eventually the character has to tell me."

—*Elmore Leonard*

Specialized Language

Write a paragraph using language or providing factual information known and understood by one or more of your characters but that is likely to be new to most of your readers.

Technical vocabulary can help your authority as a writer in fiction as well as in nonfiction. Your court stenographer character will be more believable if you, too, can talk authoritatively about daily copy, CAT transcription, hi-boy tripods, certification of questions, and deposition billing issues. In addition, arcane language can be beautiful and engrossing in its own right.

"Read a lot and hit the streets. A writer who doesn't keep up with what's out there ain't gonna be out there."

—*Toni Cade Bambara*

The Dark Before the Dawn

Even if your novel is going to end happily, there will still be times when things seem to be hopeless, when the forces working against the protagonist seem to have prospered.

Write the scene where the protagonist is at her lowest point. Holden Caulfield's nadir, in *The Catcher in the Rye*, probably comes near the end of the book when, hiding from his parents and disappointed by a meeting with his former English teacher, he spends a miserable night in the waiting room at Grand Central Station.

Talking about his novel *The Mezzanine*, in which the main action is the narrator's lunchtime trip to a drugstore to buy shoelaces, Nicholson Baker says, "I felt that I had been mistaken in the way I'd been going about trying to write novels. I would start with a hero who was in a certain setting, and then the plot would crank into motion. All of a sudden, all of the things that I was interested in would be marginalized. Eventually I gave up on the plot part. I just had him go through his lunch hour because that seemed the most efficient way to say the things I had saved up to say. The plot has to be very tiny for me to pay any attention to it for some reason. As soon as my narrators focus on something, they seem to lose track of the fact that they're supposed to be part of some momentous chain of events."

Climax

The climax is the place where tension is highest, where the outcome of the most important plot element is decided. In a couple of paragraphs, describe the incidents that will make up the climax of your book. You might find yourself saying, "But I have a lot of climaxes!" Nevertheless, carefully choose one to sketch here. Usually, the book's true climax will be the final crisis, or moment of very high tension. If possible, it's a good idea to identify your climax early in the writing process. Doing so will help you include whatever preparation and foreshadowing you need to build to your climax, rather than require the addition of missing elements later.

John Kennedy Toole's Pulitzer prize–winning novel, *A Confederacy of Dunces*, like most novels, contains a number of tense moments. The most important plot element, however, is the protagonist Ignatius J. Reilly's desire to avoid keeping a job, in order to write his philosophical treatise on the decline of civilization. Finally, Ignatius' mother decides to have him committed to a mental institution. The arrival of the ambulance to take Ignatius away marks the beginning of the climax: Will Ignatius be institutionalized, probably forever, or will he find a way to escape?

"With me, stories and novels can start anywhere. But on the level of writing, when I begin to write, the story has been turning around in me for a long time, sometimes for weeks. But not in a way that's clear; it's a sort of general idea of the story. A house where there's a red plant in one corner, and then I know that there's an old man who walks around in this house, and that's all I know. It happens like that. And then there are the dreams, because during that time my dreams are full of references and allusions to what is going to be in the story. . . . But in general they are fragments of references. That is, my subconscious is in the process of working through a story. The story is being written inside there. So when I say that I begin anywhere, it's because I don't know what is the beginning or the end." —*Julio Cortazar*

Good and Bad

Ask ten people to describe the most despicable fictional character they can imagine, and you'll get ten different answers, because different people often have such distinct ideas of good and evil. Think about the standards of good and bad in your novel. Do your important characters live by a specific moral or religious code? If so, how easy will it be for your readers to relate to your characters' moral values?

In *Mansfield Park*, a group of young people rehearse a play called *Lovers' Vows*, despite knowing that most serious adults would disapprove of the play's subject matter. Other writers might easily have forgiven the amateur actors, but neither Jane Austen nor protagonist Fanny Price can condone the actors' mild rebelliousness. Through Austen's guidance and her skillful portrayal of Fanny, we come to empathize with Fanny when she refuses to take part in the play, although in this case her moral standards are probably quite different from our own.

Divide your characters among the categories listed below. Below each character's name, write your reason for placing him where you did. The goal of the exercise is to help clarify your novel's unique moral system—as well as to help you answer the question of whether you might have too many overly negative characters, or too many overly positive ones.

MOSTLY EVIL   **SOMEWHAT EVIL**   **SOMEWHAT GOOD**   **MOSTLY GOOD**

"If I weren't a moralist I might behave even worse than I do in ordinary life. I think—and this goes back to dad and mom and so on, if you like—that because of my strong views that some kinds of behavior are admirable and some are despicable, hence I have this fairly rare phenomenon that there are good and bad characters. And very often they're not at the center of the stage, but minor characters who are completely good (Moti in *The Anti-Death League*, for instance) and completely bad (Dr. Best)." —*Kingsley Amis*

Theme

A novel's theme is its central idea, which the events of the plot are meant to explore and illustrate. Write a few paragraphs exploring the central idea of your novel (as opposed to its subject, or its plot). Consider your main theme as well as any secondary themes, since most novels will have more than one. Then explain what characters and plot elements would lead the reader to appreciate and understand your theme.

The *plot* of Leo Tolstoy's *The Death of Ivan Ilych*, for example, details the mistakes Ivan Ilych has made during the course of his life; there are events describing his lack of compassion toward others, his unkindness to his wife, his obsession with money, his overeagerness to impress his employers. The book's *theme*, on the other hand, is Tolstoy's more universal declaration of the importance of atoning for your sins and misjudgments before the end of your life.

"I feel that the novel has to be written *about* something, so that I can answer the question in my own mind: 'this novel is about—'; whereas a short story can be a situation, a character, an incident. I do feel that novels have to have themes. I don't think short stories do." —*Mary Gordon*

Types of Endings

In the same way that there are a variety of general strategies for beginning a book, so are there different methods of coming to an end. You may decide to answer every possible question about what is going to happen to your characters, or you may tease the reader by leaving a loose end or two.

Even if you've already thought about some possible endings, do this exercise as a way of exploring possibilities. After the examples below, describe a conclusion to your own novel that follows the guidelines of each of the categories.

Complete Finality, No Loose Ends Left. In this kind of ending, there's no doubt that solutions—positive or negative—to all problems have been found. At the end of Herman Wouk's *The Caine Mutiny*, we know just about everything there is to know about what is going to happen next. We know that the mutineers have been exonerated, that Captain Queeg's military career is over, and that the hero, Willie Keith, much matured, will be reunited forever with his girlfriend.

Some Important Outcomes Left to the Imagination. In Margaret Mitchell's *Gone With the Wind,* Scarlett O'Hara has finally realized that it's Rhett Butler she loves. Rhett, however, has rejected Scarlett for what seems to be a last time. Scarlett believes she will be able to get Rhett back, and since, after all, she always has been able to before, she may well have a point. As readers, though, we can't know for sure.

Circular Ending. Sometimes it's likely that the circumstances leading to the situation of the novel will occur again later. In Albert Camus' *The Plague*, the townspeople of Oran are jubilant that the bubonic plague epidemic is finally over. Only the novel's protagonist knows "that the plague bacillus never dies or disappears for good; that it can lie dormant for years and years in furniture and linen-chests."

Enormous Changes. In this kind of an ending, the situation is pretty much opposite the situation at the beginning. Ford Madox Ford's *The Good Soldier* begins with the protagonist believing that his wife was a good woman who died of a heart attack; he describes their seemingly happy, privileged life rather smugly. At the end of the book, he has realized that his wife was unfaithful to him at every opportunity and committed suicide to avoid his discovery.

Surprise Ending. Three women in Margaret Atwood's *The Robber Bride* have spent much of their lives hating their former friend Zenia for seducing their husbands and boyfriends. They finally decide to confront Zenia together but, to their shock, find her dead, apparently a suicide. It's a fitting end to the novel—but not a predictable one.

"There is no point asserting and reasserting what the heart cannot believe." —*Aleksandr Isayevich Solzhenitsyn*

Dénouement

Describe what is going to happen after the climactic moment of your book. Probably, you won't be able to stop immediately after the climax; there will be loose ends to tie up.

Steven Millhauser's novel *Edwin Mullhouse* is narrated by Edwin's ten-year-old friend Jeffrey. Most of the novel centers on Edwin's plan to kill himself on his eleventh birthday, and, with Jeffrey's help, he finally does this. The suicide is the climax of the book. Afterward, though, there's some mopping up to do: We learn that Edwin's family moves away and Jeffrey, lonely, begins spending most of his playtime with his younger sister and writing Edwin's biography. That's the book's dénouement, and you'll probably need one for your own novel.

"When you write a novel, there's really only one way to decide which of the thousands of novels you might write that you are going to write at this time. What you do is that you write the kind of novel that you yourself would want to read at that particular time." — *Vance Bourjaily*

Possibilities

Crowds

Write a scene in which your goal is to present the mood of a crowd—at least twenty people in a small space. Here, you'll include a lot of characters, but it may turn out that none of them is mentioned again in your novel.

You may use either dialogue or exposition to create your effect. Here is Nick Carraway's description of a few of Gatsby's party guests in *The Great Gatsby*.

> From East Egg, then, came the Chester Beckers and the Leeches, and a man named Bunsen, whom I knew at Yale, and Doctor Webster Civet, who was drowned last summer up in Maine. And the Hornbeams and the Willie Voltaires, and a whole clan named Blackbuck, who always gathered in a corner and flipped up their noses like goats at whosoever came near. And the Ismays and the Chrysties (or rather Hubert Auerbach and Mr. Chrystie's wife), and Edgar Beaver, whose hair, they say, turned cotton-white one winter afternoon for no good reason at all.

"No one put a gun to your head and ordered you to become a writer. One writes out of his own choice and must be prepared to take the rough spots along the road with a certain equanimity, though allowed some grinding of teeth." —*Stanley Ellin*

Development and Degeneration

Show your character in some action at the end of the book that she never would have engaged in, because it would have been against her better judgment or moral convictions, at the beginning.

Just as the external circumstances of your main characters' lives are going to change during the course of the novel, it's likely that they're going to change internally as well. The change can be for the better, as it is with Scrooge in Charles Dickens' *A Christmas Carol*; or it can be for the worse, as it is with the greedy Clyde Griffiths, who plans to kill his pregnant girlfriend in Theodore Dreiser's *An American Tragedy*.

"I don't plan until I sit down. I'm a really intuitive writer—no plan, no end point—so I can have all the ideas in the world, but until I sit down at the keyboard, I have no idea whether I've got a live fish on the line or not. I wait for my books to write themselves; the conscious mind doesn't really know much about getting that to happen on a schedule." —*Gish Jen*

Obnoxious Characters

One of the main joys of novel writing can be in the creation of obnoxious characters, people whose behavior the reader can despise, or laugh at, or simply be contemptuous of. Write a monologue in which a character reveals more of himself than he realizes, in a negative way, through his speech. You're looking for someone who *thinks* he's making himself look good but in fact is not.

Here, in William Wharton's *Birdy*, the protagonist's unpleasant father explains that he has just sold his son's car.

> "Your Uncle Nicky come over with one of his 'friends' and the friend wanted the car; he thought it'd be a real gag and offered me a C note. What'd ya think I'm gonna do anyhow; get myself in trouble over some junk heap of a car?"

Outsiders

Write a scene about a character who is an outsider, by virtue of race, religion, sexual orientation, intelligence, language, economic status, beliefs, or personality. Try to make your outsider character—as well as reactions to your outsider character—psychologically interesting and original.

Lucy Snow in Charlotte Brontë's *Villette* is an outsider at the Belgian boarding school where she teaches English. She is a Protestant, English-speaking woman in a society of French-speaking Catholics. She's considered dull and insignificant by most of the other characters, even other native English speakers. Her isolation, however, builds her character, and she finds happiness with an eccentric professor who she believes has ascertained her true personality, calling her arrogant, egotistical, weak, and "coquette comme dix Parisiennes."

Asked about American expatriates as a theme, Edmund White says, "I think it's a good theme. I'm not the first to do it, naturally. James, Wharton, Hemingway, Stein and so many other American writers have written about this. The theme enables me to work within a certain literary tradition and allows me to represent the way people are living now. Americans living in the United States are so chauvinistic. They tend to think people should only want to live in their country. This is not so in cities like Paris, where every third person is an expatriate from somewhere."

Family Tree

If your novel includes a lot of related characters, consider including a family tree or some other kind of diagram to help the reader keep everyone straight in his mind. Indeed, a family tree will also keep relationships straight in your own mind. Vladimir Nabokov includes a family tree at the beginning of *Ada*, which not only helps the reader keep track of four generations of characters, but also emphasizes the importance of the close and complicated blood ties of the three main characters, Van, Ada, and Lucette.

Create a chart showing the relationships between your characters. Your diagram may end up as an actual part of your novel, but it doesn't have to. If another kind of diagram is more useful (for example, if none of your characters is related, but all work together in an office), try that instead.

After the last page of his 1995 novel, *The End of Vandalism*, Tom Drury lists the name and profession of all of his characters, in order of their appearance in the book. If most of your characters are members of the class of 1964, for example, you might make a list followed by a few descriptive words about their class ranks and other kinds of material that might appear in a high school yearbook.

CHARACTERS
(in order of appearance)

Dan Norman, county sheriff

Louise Darling, photographer's assistant

Charles (Tiny) Darling, thief

Earl Kellogg, Jr., senior deputy sheriff

Ed Aiken, junior deputy sheriff

Rollie Wilson, ambulance driver

Henry Hamilton, notary public

Jerry Tate, postal worker

Paul Francis, crop duster

Mrs. Thorsen, science teacher

Something From the News

Write a scene in which your characters are affected by a real-life event, something you know about from the news.

Some novels completely ignore the world outside—and perhaps with good reason. On the other hand, references to current events can both ground and enrich your novel. Even if you're not writing historical fiction, an event from the news or from history can play a role. Joyce Maynard's *To Die For* is based on a news story involving the murder of a schoolteacher's husband by her teenage boyfriend. Kurt Vonnegut's *Slaughterhouse Five* describes the destruction of Dresden, Germany, during World War II. Although Bobbie Ann Mason's *In Country* takes place in the mid-1980s, the Vietnam War still looms large; the protagonist's father was killed in the war, and her uncle was debilitated by Agent Orange.

"I think life itself is so interesting you don't need to invent anything. I couldn't possibly hope to better it. Usually I base the story on newspaper headlines. Like two sisters murder their mother. Well, I never follow the case up. I just find an incident I want to write about. I don't know how it will turn out until I write it." —*Beryl Bainbridge*

What About the Bomb?

Are there big issues about which you feel strongly? Nuclear power? Abortion? Gun control? The legalization of drugs? Animal rights? Welfare reform? Write a scene in which you try to convince the reader—without being too preachy—of one of your own deeply held beliefs.

Didactic, or "thesis," novels—novels whose intent is to convince the reader to take a particular point of view—are not easy to write and, when they don't work, are often disdained. But when a novel with a moral does work—when it is well written and engrossing—no one is going to complain. Ralph Ellison's *Invisible Man* is in part meant to show how African-Americans need to find strength within themselves to fight their battles and not count on other groups to fight for them. Because the characters and scenes are so intense and memorable, no one would think of calling the novel didactic in the negative sense.

". . . when I was in Peru recently, someone asked me an extraordinary question at a lecture I gave. All the questions had been very literary—informed, thoughtful. There were writers there, and academics. It was a civilized audience with elegant manners. And this guy piped up and said, 'When are you going to write about the neutron bomb?' Everyone was embarrassed. But it was a good question. 'I've been writing about the neutron bomb all my life,' I told him. And in one way I have. But what he was talking about was, What are you going to do *now*? How can you feel (and I don't, of course) that anyone's written anything since it's still there? It's your bomb! When are you going to write about it?"—*E.L. Doctorow*

Animals

Write a scene in which one of your characters interacts with an animal. This can be his own pet, someone else's pet, a stray, a wild animal—any non-anthropomorphized animal you'd like to use.

People often let their guards down in their relations with animals and reveal sides of their characters—good and bad—they are reluctant to reveal to other people. In Carson McCullers' *Reflections in a Golden Eye*, the not-that-likable character Private Elgee Williams shows a sympathetic side of his personality by his treatment of a pregnant mare.

> The young soldier took from his pocket an envelope of sugar and soon his hands were warm and sticky with slaver. He went into the stall of a little mare who was almost ready to drop her foal. He stroked her swollen belly and stood for a time with his arms around her neck.

Another character's hypersensitivity—and her husband's crassness—is revealed as she caresses a dead bird.

> She held the little warm, ruffled body that had somehow become degraded in its fall, and looked into the head's little glassy black eyes. Then she burst into tears. This was the sort of thing the Major meant by "female" and "morbid"; and it did a man no good to figure it out.

"Whether we are describing a king, an assassin, a thief, an honest man, a prostitute, a nun, a young girl, or a stallholder in a market, it is always ourselves that we are describing." —*Guy de Maupassant*

Juxtaposing Elements

Think about two different emotions and moods (misery? malicious glee?), emotions not likely to occur in the same person at the same time. Then think of two situations likely to evoke different emotions from characters (a speech by William McKinley? a horrible avalanche?) and from readers. Find a way to merge these disparate elements in a single, unified scene.

Tony Hillerman's *The Listening Woman* opens with a scene in which a seriously ill man is visited by a Navajo healer and her sixteen-year-old assistant, Anna Atcitty. Anna has just painted a "colorful curved stick figure of the Rainbow Man" on the man's chest "in the ritual tints of blue, yellow, green and gray." It's a scene evoking mystery and magic. But we also read the words on Anna's T-shirt, "GANADO HIGH SCHOOL" and "TIGER PEP," and are flooded with images of an ordinary contemporary teenager. The juxtaposition of the mysterious and the everyday is what makes the scene—and Anna—so haunting and memorable. And it's important that we learn to care about Anna quickly, because she's about to be murdered, and the rest of the book concerns the search for her killer.

"I've got a kind of theory, that while it's hard for people to believe murder and this stuff, if you give them a realistic setting in which all this takes place, where there's a half-empty bowl of oatmeal on the table and children catching school buses, it makes the events seem less Hollywoodish, more down-to-earth and real-life."

—*Tony Hillerman*

Documents

Create a document written by a character in your novel (a job application or résumé? a high school paper? a list of New Year's resolutions? a peculiar grocery list?) that the character does not mean for anyone else to see. Your goal is to explore some aspect of the character that would not be clear through the portrayal of his thoughts and actions alone.

In Charles Newman's *There Must Be More to Love Than Death*, the soldier protagonist George Patek visits the public library in a small town where he is stationed. When Patek tries to apply for a library card, the librarian hands him this document.

Summer Reading Program

ELIGIBILITY: Ability to read (even 1st graders may enter).
Each reader goes along at own speed and ALL readers are winners!

REGISTRATION:
One book—
Reader submits a report written briefly in the library during regular 0900-1700 hours, and is enrolled as a **"Ranch Hand"** in the club. Report is filed in manuscript folder to be given back to reader at end of summer, together with appropriate awards for quantity and quality of reading done.

ADVANCEMENT:
Three books—
Reader receives an emblem representing work done on the ranch—one emblem for each book read and recorded in permanent record book. Third book denotes promotion to full ranking **"Cowboy."**

Five books—
Reader receives emblem for each book indicating work accomplished as a **cowboy** (branding calves, roping steers, etc.). Fifth book denotes graduation to **"Bronc-buster"** class.

Eight books—
Reader receives "ribbons" for skills in rodeo competition—eighth ribbon denotes graduation to **"Ranch Owner"** class.
Ranch Owners may do **anything,** so reader will hang up his own private ranch chart, select his private ranch brand, and receive, for each book read, an emblem representing any task or skill that he wishes.

*Party at end of summer for presentation of awards
and certificates*

The notice George receives would be funny even out of the context of the novella, which is presented in part as a set of military documents relating to the investigation of a crime that George has committed. In addition, the patronizing set of hoops through which George must jump before getting his library card serves as a symbol of George's increasing frustration and alienation with Air Force life.

In this excerpt from *The Adrian Mole Diaries,* by Sue Townsend, Adrian presents his own list along with his mother's list of possible names for the baby Adrian's mother is expecting. The lists say something about the romantic natures of the characters, as well as the way in which they have been influenced by popular culture (Is Adrian thinking of La Toya Jackson? Princess Diana? Georgina from the *Upstairs, Downstairs* TV series?).

My mothers' [sic]: Charity, Christobel, Zoe, Jade, Frankie, India, Rosie, Caitlin, Ruth
Mine: Tracy, Claire, Toyah, Diana, Pandora, Sharon, Georgina

"Novelists and short story writers provide implicitly a critique of their society." —Nadine Gordimer

Coincidence

Write a scene in which coincidence plays a key role.

Writers tend to be wary of coincidence—the lottery ticket that saves the family farm, the judge who turns out to have committed the murder for which the protagonist is on trial. Most writers prefer to find a conclusion based on the logical actions of the characters and their abilities to find (or not to find) solutions to their problems.

But don't underestimate the role of chance. In Nancy Mitford's *Love in a Cold Climate*, Polly's mother is furious that her beautiful daughter has not yet fallen in love with anyone, despite the approaching end of her debutante year. Polly has wisely told no one of her passion for her uncle-by-marriage. Then Polly's aunt dies suddenly, leaving the uncle unattached at last. The novel could have ended soon after this coincidence, with a big wedding and happiness for all. What really happens, though, is that Polly's parents change their will, and Polly and the uncle, low on money for the first time ever, become rapidly disenchanted with each other.

The lesson we can take from this is that coincidence that solves the characters' problems and ties up the plot too neatly will often seem contrived, while coincidence that affects the characters in less happy ways is often an appropriate and useful way to move your plot forward.

"If you study the history of literature, you see that certain art forms decline and others arise. In the seventeenth century, the novel was considered a trashy, low, literary form, suitable for serving-maids who wanted to pervert their minds." —*Erica Jong*

Hold Something Back

Reveal a secret about one of your characters that you have been keeping from your readers.

The narrator of Agatha Christie's mystery *The Murder of Roger Ackroyd*, for example, reveals at the end of the novel that he himself committed the crime, during a few moments in which he was vague in describing his whereabouts to the reader. In Chuck Palahniuk's *Fight Club*, the narrator asserts his allegiance to Project Mayhem, a deranged movement designed to bring anarchy to the city and "break up civilization so we can make something better out of the world." For most of the novel the reader believes the leader of Project Mayhem to be a psychopath named Tyler Durden, who has brainwashed the protagonist into blowing up a 191-story skyscraper. It's not until three-quarters of the way through the book that the writer reveals that Tyler Durden and the protagonist are actually the same person, that Tyler Durden is a kind of alternate personality who exists only in the protagonist's mind.

"People who write are driven. Otherwise nobody would do it. I mean, I was warned when I began writing that it was very, very hard. I thought it was easy. I thought, well, you don't have to show up anywhere and go to work, and you can make up stories, and so forth. But I was warned, rightly, that it was very, very hard work. All writers who regularly write, I think, are driven." —*Robert Stone*

Recognition

A *recognition*, as defined by the Greek philosopher Aristotle, involves a character's discovery of a fact that, while true all along, has not been known previously. In John Fowles' *The French Lieutenant's Woman*, the mysterious woman, who has led everyone to believe she was the mistress of the French lieutenant, turns out not to have been the mistress of anyone at all. This discovery is an example of a recognition. Another recognition, in Charles Dickens' *Great Expectations*, comes when Pip, who has cast off his humble family after receiving money from a benefactor, is distressed to discover that his benefactor is Abel Magwitch, an escaped convict.

Write a recognition: Reveal a truth that has been kept secret, either by happenstance or through the deceit of the characters involved, through most of the novel.

"I shall live bad if I do not write and I shall write bad if I do not live." — Françoise Sagan

Reversal

Another Aristotelian concept is the *reversal*. This is an act that results in consequences that are the direct opposite of those hoped for by the person performing the action. In Benjamin Cheever's *The Plagiarist*, the protagonist, the son of a famous writer, writes a story in the style of his father, signs his father's name to it, and submits it to the magazine where the son works. His goal is to find happiness and advance his career by bringing in new work by his legendarily difficult, reclusive father. However, while the plagiarism is not detected at the magazine, his guilt and shame make him feel the opposite of the joy he had expected.

Write a scene that involves a reversal, an action by a character that brings about the opposite effect of what he wanted.

"If you're a good writer, you will lose all of the readers of the present book that you gained with the previous book, because you will always be changing." —*Paul Valéry*

The Internal Plot

A novel, unlike a short story, is probably going to have more than one plot. One way of plotting is to contrast an active, external plot with a more introspective, meditative one involving some sort of internal change in the protagonist. Ernest Hemingway's *The Sun Also Rises* offers both an internal plot (Jake Barnes' struggle to find inner peace despite the knowledge that he'll never be able to have Brett Ashley) and an external plot (Jake Barnes' trip to Spain to fish and watch the bulls).

Think about your own novel and briefly sketch a plot that involves your main character in both an external, active quest and an internal, mental, or psychological struggle.

"I think the only person a writer has an obligation to is himself. If what I write doesn't fulfill something in me, if I don't honestly feel it's the best I can do, then I'm miserable." — *Truman Capote*

A Plot of Contrasts

Most novels have either a main plot and one or more subplots, or several main plots of equal importance. Very often, it's a good idea for these plots to differ dramatically from one another in important ways, involving, for example, different types of characters or situations.

External plot vs. internal plot (as described on page 80) is just one way to use contrast. Your contrasting plots might include sets of characters of different social classes or lifestyles; or a personal plot involving the lives of human beings might contrast with a less personal, more issue-oriented plot; or one plotline could be tragic and the other basically comic. In *Anna Karenina*, Leo Tolstoy contrasts the plot of Anna Karenina's decline as she commits adultery with Aleksei Vronsky with the uplifting plot of Konstantin Levin as he finds joy living the simple life of a peasant worker on his estate.

Keeping your primary plotline in mind, sketch two or three possible contrasting plotlines, involving different characters, locations, moods, or themes.

"I like density, not volume. I like to leave something to the imagination. The reader must fit the pieces together, with the author's discreet help." —*Maureen Howard*

Flashbacks

Even if the action of your novel takes place mainly in 1984, your character might at some point remember in vivid detail an important event that happened in 1918. Indeed, it's a rare novel that doesn't include at least a short flashback. Write a scene showing something that happened to one of your characters before the opening of the book. Your goal is to reveal to the reader what kind of person that character was before the time of the novel.

The final chapter of Richard Yates' *A Good School* takes place in 1955. In it, the protagonist, William Grove, thinks with gratitude about how his prep school years prepared him for his career as a newspaperman. Then, suddenly Yates has his narrator flash back to a period before the novel's beginning, in which Grove imagines his father as a younger man.

> All I'm really qualified to remember is the sadness of his later life—the bad marriage that cost him so much, the drab little office from which he assisted in managing the sales of light bulbs for so many years, the tidy West Side apartment, redolent of lamb stew, where I can only hope he found love before his death.

After musing about his father, Grove returns to 1955. Through this sad, powerful image of Grove's long-dead father, who has up to now seemed a bit of a buffoon, we come to see both characters in completely new ways.

"I've watched television all my life, and I think my way of editing, the speed I bring to my books, the way the plot moves, is based upon some of the television shows and cartoons I've seen, the way they edit. Look at a late movie that was made in 1947—people become bored because there was a slower tempo in those times."

—*Ishmael Reed*

Flash-Forwards

Write a flash-forward; your narrator looks ahead to a specific moment in the future, allows the reader to learn about events your character could not possibly predict, and then returns to the present. If your novel is written in the first person, let the character describe a specific future event as if he had the ability to see into the future. This exercise differs from the one on page 96, "The Effects of Time," because in that exercise you're giving a summary of the important events that will occur in your characters after the book ends; here, you're writing a particular scene that will actually appear in your novel.

Gabriel García Márquez's *One Hundred Years of Solitude* opens this way.

> Many years later, as he faced the firing squad, Colonel Aureliano Buendía was to remember that distant afternoon when his father took him to discover ice.

Immediately after this look into the future, the action switches back to the novel's present time, when Aureliano Buendía is only six years old. The firing-squad episode doesn't occur until a quarter of the way into the book, but because we know about it in advance, everything that occurs before it is shadowed by our belief that the character is destined for an early, violent death.

"My advice for beginning writers is first to recognize that writers differ a great deal in their own natures and in the nature of their talent, and that little advice which is general can be of much value. Learn not to take advice. Look to yourself. Make yourself worthy of trust." —*William Gass*

Sex

Write a sex scene between two of your characters. If none of your characters is romantically involved with any other, write a fantasy that takes place in a character's mind. Be as explicit as you want in the language. You might find it useful as an exercise, though, to try Toni Morrison's suggestion and describe the entire encounter without naming actual body parts.

It might be useful to take a few minutes to review the sexiest scenes in novels you own, even trashy ones, and think about what makes those scenes memorable—this passage from Colleen McCullough's *Tim*, for example.

> The kiss was different from their first, it had a languorous sensuality about it that Mary found fey and witching, as if the creature she had surprised dreaming was not Tim at all, but a manifestation of the soft summer night. Rising from the balcony railing without fear or hesitation, he pulled her into his arms and picked her up.

Is it the surprising "fey and witching," combined with the vagueness of the actual description of Tim, that seems suggestive? Is it the fecund, fertile atmosphere in the garden where Tim carries Mary? Tim's impressive strength?

"If I want the reader to feel sexy when I describe a sexual scene, such as with Ajax and Sula, I will provide the broadstrokes: he is horizontal, she is vertical. And there is no sexy language in there at all. I think 'breast' is really the only physical word. While they are making love, he isn't saying anything that you can hear, but she is thinking things that have to do with loam and stuff. Nothing scatological. I rely on the readers' awareness of something that is much more primitive—mud—which is something you associate with childhood when 'dirt' was all right, and you could really make a mud pie. So that's the image that controls the sexual scene. The reader brings his own sexuality into it, which is always sexier than mine. That is to say, one's own sexuality is always sexier than anybody else's, because it's yours. Which is why clinical descriptions of sex are usually boring, if you have any sex life or imagination at all." —*Toni Morrison*

Travel

In fiction, as in life, a change of scene can do you good. On a journey, characters can meet new people or learn to see other characters in a different light. A trip also gives the writer a chance to describe a new environment, to inject some perhaps-needed new blood into a novel. Write a scene in which one or more of your characters takes a trip somewhere and is changed (even if only in a minor, temporary way) by the experience. It might be especially interesting to choose a destination that at first glance might seem unlikely to attract your characters.

Alice Walker's *The Color Purple*, for example, is full of journeys, but an important one comes near the end of the novel, when Celie spends a summer in Memphis with her friend Shug Avery. While there, Celie, whose life has until now been pretty miserable, finds the strength within herself to start a sewing business. Returning home, she finds that her wretched husband has missed her so much that he makes a sincere effort to treat her more considerately; he becomes an affectionate confidant to Celie for the rest of the novel.

"I am convinced that it is better for a writer to know a little bit of the world remarkably well than to know a great part of the world remarkably little." — *Thomas Hardy*

In Medias Res

Some novels start in the middle of the action, *in medias res*. This technique is often used to challenge the reader to figure out the story through the book's context rather than through formal exposition. Beginning *in medias res* can be especially useful if realism is your goal; in real life we often find ourselves thrust into situations and then having to figure out exactly what's going on. E.M. Forster's *Howards End*, for example, begins with a letter from Helen to her sister Margaret.

> Dearest Meg,
>
> It isn't going to be what we expected. It is old and little, and altogether delightful–red brick. We can scarcely pack in as it is, and the dear knows what will happen when Paul (younger son) arrives tomorrow.

At first, we have no idea what the situation is. Who is Meg? Who is writing the letter? To what does the title, *Howards End*, refer? In what way are things not as expected? The reader sorts things out gradually over the course of the next chapter.

Write a new opening for your novel that begins *in medias res*. Don't explain everything; assume that the reader, like the characters, already knows what's going on.

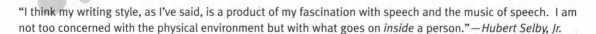

"I think my writing style, as I've said, is a product of my fascination with speech and the music of speech. I am not too concerned with the physical environment but with what goes on *inside* a person." —*Hubert Selby, Jr.*

Racing the Clock

Write a scene in which one or more of your characters must work against some specific time limit, when there will be a definite penalty if the characters do not meet their deadline.

Time is especially important in suspense novels. Think of Michael Crichton's *The Andromeda Strain:* The characters fight a computer countdown to the destruction of an underground laboratory that has been contaminated by a poisonous airborne virus.

The race against time can be important in literary novels too, as in Faulkner's *As I Lay Dying*, in which the Bundrens must get Addie buried before the buzzards get her. In Marcel Proust's *In Search of Lost Time*, the character Marcel must finish his masterpiece before dying.

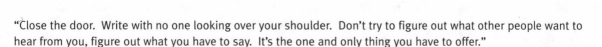

"Close the door. Write with no one looking over your shoulder. Don't try to figure out what other people want to hear from you, figure out what you have to say. It's the one and only thing you have to offer."

—*Barbara Kingsolver*

Humor

Have you read a novel so funny that remembering it makes you laugh? On the lines below, list your favorite comic novels, and think about what makes their humor so memorable.

_____   _____   _____

Now, write a few funny paragraphs to include in your own novel. Do this even if your novel isn't remotely humorous—remember the importance of comic relief. You can find humor in the absurd, or in the day-to-day occurrences of life.

"Good comic writing comes from a very nearly irrational center that stays viable because it is unexplainable. It often disports itself in a kind of charged language. That is to say it is not appropriate to use exactly the same prose style for writing an all-out comedy as it is for writing a rural tragedy. Each book demands its own stylistic answers."—*Thomas McGuane*

Housekeeping

Write a few paragraphs describing the way one (or more) of your characters keeps house, and then explain what the character's housekeeping says about him (or them).

In Anne Tyler's *The Accidental Tourist*, the fussy characters alphabetize the contents of their kitchen cabinets. In Marilynne Robinson's *Housekeeping*, on the other hand, home management declines quickly when Sylvie takes over.

> The kitchen was stacked with cans, and with brown paper bags. Sylvie knew that such collecting invited mice, so she brought home a yellow cat with half an ear and a bulging belly, and it littered twice. The first litter was old enough already to prey on the swallows that had begun to nest on the second floor. This was good and useful, but the cats often brought the birds into the parlor, and left wings and feet and heads lying about, even on the couch.

Notice how Robinson's psychology doesn't become overly simplistic. Do the baby clothes of the ten-year-old son of your characters, still scattered on the floor in the dining room, signify the parents' pathological sloppiness, or suggest an admirable indifference to convention? Might the baby clothes symbolize the mother's sorrow at the end of an important life stage? Is the messiness a rebellion against the father's overly neat upbringing?

"I tried in *Housekeeping* to speak fairly respectfully of the whole phenomenon of housekeeping. The grandmother, in particular, is a sort of artist in that form. I don't intend to create oppositions. In a way, Sylvie's housekeeping is a sort of variant of other people's housekeeping, in the sense that what is really accomplished in terms of accumulating things that matter and stabilizing environments and so on, is on a range between unsuccessful and even less successful. It's not as if anybody succeeds at this. It's just that Sylvie's failures are more obvious."

—*Marilynne Robinson*

Repeated Stories

Write an anecdote that you could include in your novel more than once.

In real life, people repeat themselves a lot. A novelist trying to create a realistic view of life might wish to capture some of that repetition of speech. *In The Making of Americans*, Gertrude Stein confides that when she finds a character "baffling," she listens to the ways he repeats himself.

You can have a character repeat an anecdote to show the reader how boring he is, but repetition can do more than that: The story itself can change over time, or the reader or other characters might only after the third time realize its significance. In Agatha Christie's *The Mirror Crack'd*, the garrulous Heather Badcock tells an actress about getting out of bed during an illness many years before to shake her hand. After Heather Badcock's murder, the apparently insignificant story is retold several times by different characters before its significance is realized: The actress had suddenly realized Heather Badcock infected her with rubella while she was pregnant, resulting in her child's birth defects.

"How can you write if you can't cry?"—*Ring Lardner*

Symbols

A symbol is an object that represents something else as well as itself. In Gloria Naylor's *Linden Hills*, for example, a normally kind and gentle character is periodically consumed by a demented rage that he calls "the pinks." "The pinks" as a form of mental illness is certainly fascinating on a literal level, but it also symbolizes the destructive influence of white people on blacks in America. A symbol doesn't need to be as obvious as "the pinks," and frequently symbols will come into existence through the writer's subconscious rather than conscious process. Other times, readers will become aware of symbols that the writer did not even intend. Often, symbols will be generated from the same kind of charged images (see pages 4–5) that generated the ideas for the novel in the first place.

List and describe any symbols or sets of symbols in your novel, and explain what they symbolize. Particularly if you haven't yet thought about using symbols, write a scene that includes an object that exists on a literal level and also works as a kind of shorthand for or echo of some larger concept or idea.

"What's happened recently is that writers are using the machinery of the fable but without wishing to point a simple moral. I don't think of either *Midnight's Children* or *Shame* as containing a moral. *Shame* is about ethics, about good and evil, but it doesn't tell you how to behave, whereas fable does. *Shame* is not morally didactic; it shows you something. Italo Calvino is described as a fabulist, but his stories don't have morals: they're shaped like fables, they have the characteristics of fables, but without the purpose." — *Salman Rushdie*

Diaries

Write a diary entry, meant to be private, in which one of your characters describes, with total honesty, an event and his feelings about the event.

You might also want to go back to any diaries, as opposed to writer's journals (see page 9), you have kept. Highlight or put Post-it Notes on the most evocative, memorable passages. Are there portions you could excerpt in your novel?

If you don't currently keep a private diary, consider starting one. Your entries certainly don't have to end up in your novel, but the habit of frequent, objective reflection might be useful. It can be a relief—and an inspiration—to write without a critical audience in mind. Still, Gail Godwin believes most diary writers write "for *some* form of audience. This audience may be God, or it may be a friendly (or unfriendly) spirit (witness the way some diarists must justify their self-contradictions and shortcomings); or it may be one's future self (at thirty-eight, Virginia Woolf wrote in her journal that she was hoping to entertain herself at fifty)."

"A man is not idle because he is absorbed in thought; there is a visible labor and there is an invisible labor."
— *Victor Hugo*

When You're Stuck

A Really Bad Day

It's frustrating when you've cleared time to write, sent the family out of town, sat down at the computer—and nothing comes of it. Do this exercise after you've had a bad writing day, but only as a last resort, when you're completely sure you can't work on your novel.

First, see how much you actually did write, and try to assess the quality of the work. John Steinbeck writes, "I do a whole of a day's work and then the next day, flushed with triumph, I dawdle. . . . The crazy thing is that I get about the same number of words down either way." A day when the writing's not as enjoyable as usual isn't necessarily a bad day. Note also how long you were stopped. A five-minute interruption is not a big deal; twenty-five five-minute interruptions probably are. Remember that every writer has to work through some false starts. Don't beat yourself up if the scene you wrote today isn't actually going to end up in your novel or if your rough draft seems rougher than usual.

REASONS FOR A BAD WRITING DAY

____ necessary interruption (fire in yard)

____ seminecessary interruption (paid fifteen overdue bills—yes, but why during your writing time?)

____ unnecessary interruption (neighbor wants to borrow ant traps)

____ technical malfunction (coffee spilled on chapter seven)

____ unnecessary digression (spent day figuring out how to create footnotes in WordPerfect)

____ stupid distraction (solitaire)

____ disorganized work space (misplaced chapter five; spent afternoon looking for it)

____ maddening irritants (noisy construction work outside; if this is chronic, have you tried earplugs?)

____ illness (chronic or temporary? cold? flu? hypochondria?)

____ need for sleep (did you nap? how long?)

____ no writing ideas (try a writing exercise!)

____ just couldn't concentrate (how long did you try? what did you do instead?)

____ bored by characters (which ones? why?)

____ wrote scene, then realized it was a bad one

____ just can't figure out what should happen next

____ know what should happen next, but something (the embarrassing nature of the event? the difficulty of researching a skiing scene in the summer?) is holding you back from actually writing the scene

_____ wrote something unrelated to novel (letter to newspaper? résumé? was it worth the time?)

_____ felt guilty spending the day writing rather than doing "real" work

_____ discouraging comments from "friends" or teachers have you too upset to continue

_____ worry about non-writing-related problems makes it too hard to work right now

_____ losing confidence in the whole idea of the novel

_____ spent day doing research but didn't find what you wanted

_____ an unexpected and enjoyable nonwriting option appeared

_____ other (what? _____)

Write as clearly, specifically, and honestly as possible about why you've had a bad writing day rather than a good one. If you're having trouble writing because you're sick of your novel and your characters, you might need to rethink some important aspect, or perhaps you're just working through a difficult but necessary stage in the writing process.

Now, describe how you can avoid these obstacles in the future. If you can't avoid them, how can you work around them? Are there obstacles you can avoid (stay away from negative people; organize your work space during non-writing time) or will someone else have to help (explain to your neighbor that you can't find the ant traps now, but you'll be glad to look for them later)?

"Being a real writer means being able to work on a bad day." —_Norman Mailer_

The Effects of Time

Imagine one of your characters twenty or forty years after the end of your novel. What will he be doing? Write a scene in which your protagonist or another character appears. Have the events of your novel affected him at all? Has he prospered or failed? Have his decisions been wise?

Bernard Malamud's *Pictures of Fidelman* consists of six stories that form a coming-of-age novel about a young painter who goes through a variety of humiliating experiences before realizing that while he was not meant to be an artist, he still must struggle to become a better human being. Malamud writes, "I was out to loosen up—experiment a little—with narrative structure. And I wanted to see, if I wrote it at intervals—as I did from 1957 to 1968—whether the passing of time and mores would influence his life."

"Time, when it is left to itself and no definite demands are made on it, cannot be trusted to move at any recognized pace. Usually it loiters; but just when one has come to count upon its slowness, it may suddenly break into a wild, irrational gallop." —*Edith Wharton*

Write What You *Don't* Know

First novelists traditionally base their novels on personal experience, which often provides rich and wonderful material. Depending on your life, though, autobiographical fiction can be constricting. Just because you don't have firsthand-experience with a subject doesn't mean you can't write about it—although writing about an unfamiliar subject with authority is a challenge. Still, you can always do research later, if necessary.

In "The Art of Fiction," Henry James writes about an English writer.

> [She] was praised by a reader for her accurate depiction of French Protestant youth and asked how she had learned so much about the subject. The writer responded that she "once, in Paris, as she ascended a staircase, passed an open door where, in a household of a *pasteur*, some of the young Protestants were seated at table round a finished meal. The glimpse made a picture; it lasted only a moment, but that moment was experience. . . . She knew what youth was, and what Protestantism was; she also had the advantage of having seen what it was to be French, so that she converted these ideas into a concrete image and produced a reality.

Write a scene involving characters doing something (performing brain surgery? committing arson? visiting a nudist colony?) about which you know little.

"I don't try to be so very careful to limit what I write to things that I know I can do. More and more I find I'm willing to take a chance on showing bad taste and ignorance if it will allow me a new and broader expression. I try at the same time to keep an honest and intelligent eye on what are my limitations for total success in a thing. I continue to take pleasure in doing the things that are my type." —*Peter Taylor*

More Is More

One of the luxuries of being a novelist is that, unlike many short story writers, you have the space to include scenes and ideas that don't necessarily move the action forward. Write a few paragraphs that relate to your novel thematically but do not especially contribute to the linear plot—information to include simply because it's beautifully written and compelling in its own right.

Herman Melville's *Moby Dick*, for example, includes chapters describing paintings and wood carvings of whales, the spiritual significance of the whiteness of whales, and recipes for whale meat; these chapters teach us a great deal about whales but do not directly advance the plot. Ursula K. Le Guin's *Always Coming Home*, 525 pages long, includes songs, poems, stories, and recipes important to the imaginary Kesh society.

"I believe that *more* is more. I believe that less is less, fat FAT, thin thin, and enough enough. There's a famous exchange between Fitzgerald and Thomas Wolfe in which Fitzgerald criticizes Wolfe for one of his novels. Fitzgerald tells him that Flaubert believed in the *mot precis* and that there are two kinds of writers—the putter-inners and the taker-outers. Wolfe, who probably was not as good a writer as Fitzgerald but evidently wrote a better letter, said, 'Flaubert me no Flauberts. Shakespeare was a putter-inner, Melville was a putter-inner.' I can't remember who else was a putter-inner, but I'd rather be a putter-inner than a taker-outer." —*Stanley Elkin*

Mixed-Up Characters

On small pieces of paper, write the names of all the characters in your novel. Put the slips into a bag, pull out three or four, and begin immediately to write a scene that includes all of those characters. Don't cheat—don't reach into the bag over and over until you find a group of characters you'd already planned to work with. The scene must be one whose ending, as you begin writing, is a total mystery to you. Don't stop writing until the scene reaches a natural closure of some kind.

Asked whether a character ever takes hold of him and "dictates the course of the action" in a novel, Vladimir Nabokov's response in *Strong Opinions* is "What a preposterous experience! Writers who have had it must be very minor or insane." But not every writer has his novel completely planned before beginning to write, and the bringing together of characters who don't normally meet, in fiction as in life, can lead to surprising and satisfying consequences.

In an interview, Margaret Atwood remarks, "I never know how a book is going to end when I begin it. If I knew how it was going to end, I probably would not continue on. You remember, I said I had written six and a half novels. The half was one I'd thought I'd be very clever with and have it all plotted out on filing cards before I started, and you know what that did to writing the book? First of all, it made it very long, but secondly, I already knew the plot, so it was like walking through, going through the motions. It was like 'writing down' rather than 'writing.' "

Sentence Types

If you ever look at a scene and find yourself thinking, *There's something wrong here, but I'm just not sure what,* consider looking more closely at the passage's individual words and sentences. Are they too short and choppy—or too long and convoluted? Maybe your sentences should be more or less complicated, and the general flow from sentence to sentence smoother or less smooth.

From your novel, copy a passage of ten sentences or so that bothers you.

Now, count how many words there are in these ten sentences.

1._____ 2._____ 3._____ 4._____ 5._____ 6._____ 7._____ 8._____ 9._____ 10._____

Then figure
- How many words in the shortest sentence? _____
- How many words in the longest sentence? _____
- What is the average number of words per sentence? _____

Next, take a look at the ten sentences you've written.
- How many simple sentences (subject + verb, or subject + verb + object)? ("The building is pink, bright pink" [Larry Wolff, *The Boys and Their Baby*].) ____
- How many compound sentences (two simple sentences joined with a conjunction or punctuation mark)? ("The unicorn lived in a lilac wood, and she lived all alone" [Peter S. Beagle, *The Last Unicorn*].) _____
- How many complex sentences (simple sentence containing a dependent clause or phrase)? ("Long before the soldiers arrived the life forms of the valley had established a stable symbiotic balance" [John M. Del Vecchio, *The Thirteenth Valley*].) _____
- How many compound-complex sentences (compound sentence that also includes a dependent clause)? ("In the mid-summer evenings when they had tidied away the tea-things in the kitchen the two old sisters retired to the sitting-room, and there, with the two windows open to the long-legged sun, they sat in front of the pansy-leaf firescreen that hid the empty grate" [Michael McLaverty, *School for Hope*].) ____

After you have finished the exercise with your own novel, find one by another writer, and copy a passage of about ten sentences that you particularly admire.

How many words are there in each of these ten sentences you've copied down?

1._____ 2._____ 3._____ 4._____ 5._____ 6._____ 7._____ 8._____ 9._____ 10._____

- How many words in the shortest sentence? _____
- How many words in the longest sentence? _____
- What is the average number of words per sentence? _____
- How many simple sentences are there? _____
- How many compound sentences? _____
- How many complex sentences? _____
- How many compound-complex sentences? _____

Now rewrite the passage from your novel to reflect as closely as possible the number of sentence types and sentence lengths of the scene you admire. Does emulating another writer's style help you improve the problematic passage?

"A sentence is a group of words expressing a complete thought. A thought is only the beginning of an idea. A paragraph expresses an idea. A concept can be symbolized by just one word. I know this for a fact: every artist begins with a concept. He begins with an idea, whether he's a painter, a graphic artist, a plastic artist, whether he's a musician, whether he's a writer. Creative thinking is nothing more than having the concept out of which the idea grows. It doesn't matter whether you're writing a poem or a piece of prose. It begins with the idea."

—*Margaret Walker*

Write a Letter

Write a letter from one of your characters to another. Think of the possibilities: unanswered letters, letters received that go unopened for weeks; unsent letters; purloined letters; letters lost in the mail; letters received years after they were mailed; letters addressed to A but really meant for B, a member of A's household; letters full of lies; letters accidentally found. For the purpose of the exercise, postcards and E-mail count as letters. Why is your character writing a letter? What will the recipient's feelings be on receiving it?

Letters can be fun and also structurally useful. Alice Walker, in *The Color Purple*, used letters, in part, as a way "of solving a technical problem of having characters in Georgia and Africa," she says. Especially if your novel involves characters who seldom meet, or are in far-flung locations, letters can help keep your novel unified.

I often try to put my experience in the form of a story that seems to illuminate. If people find it familiar, then there is illumination. Light is an image that I am very fond of. I literally try to put some of my characters in a strong light. Another image that I use a great deal is water. I come from a seafaring family." —*John Cheever*

If Your Character Could Write

Write a poem ostensibly written by one of your characters. This exercise could be especially helpful in moving you closer to a character whose true nature is eluding you.

You don't have to choose one of your smarter, more creative characters but you should make the poem clearly show something specific about its writer—not just be an exercise in really bad writing. In *Forgetting Elena*, Edmund White reproduces a poem by a character his protagonist calls "a well-educated man devoid of talent." It begins with these lines.

> Rubies shiver and a child's impassioned hand
> Rises, touches skin the color of a wedding band

Even if the idea of writing a poem is intimidating or just not exciting to you, do it anyway. Many writers, after all, including Thomas Hardy, D.H. Lawrence, Randall Jarrell, Langston Hughes, James Dickey, Sylvia Plath, Maxine Kumin, D.M. Thomas, John Updike, Sandra Cisneros, Margaret Atwood, Joyce Carol Oates, N. Scott Momaday, Leslie Marmon Silko, Larry Woiwode, Alberto Ríos, Judith Ortiz Cofer, and Denis Johnson have published both fiction and poetry and are well respected as writers of both.

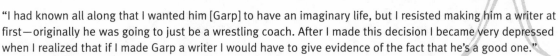

"I had known all along that I wanted him [Garp] to have an imaginary life, but I resisted making him a writer at first—originally he was going to just be a wrestling coach. After I made this decision I became very depressed when I realized that if I made Garp a writer I would have to give evidence of the fact that he's a good one."

—*John Irving*

Lies

Write a scene involving at least three characters during which at least one of the characters tells a significant lie. As you write the scene, keep the following in mind.

- How significant is the lie?
- Why has the character lied?
- Will the lie be believed?
- Will the lie be discovered?
- If it's discovered, will other characters confront the lying character, or will they let the lie pass?
- Will the lie at first go undiscovered but cause trouble for the liar later (the time-bomb lie)?

Do whatever feels right to help you write your novel, even if it might seem eccentric to others. In an interview in *The Paris Review,* Maya Angelou describes how she has written in a hotel room, in every town she's ever lived. "I rent a hotel room for a few months, leave home at six and try to be at work by 6:30. To write, I lie across the bed, so that this elbow is absolutely encrusted at the end, just so rough with callouses. I never allow the hotel people to change the bed, because I never sleep there. I stay until 12:30 or 1:30 in the afternoon, and then I go home and try to breathe; I look at the work around five; I have an orderly dinner: proper, quiet, lovely dinner; and then I go back to work the next morning. Sometimes in hotels I'll go into the room, and there'll be a note on the floor which says, 'Dear Miss Angelou, let us change the sheets. We think they are moldy.' But I only allow them to come in and empty wastebaskets. I insist that all things are taken off the walls."

Throwing Out the Bathwater

Sometimes, perhaps by happy accident, the first sentence you type will remain your first sentence forever; every character you introduce will be perfect the moment he appears; every plot twist you begin will seem worth the trouble six months later. Other times, a trail that seemed fruitful will peter out, and eventually you'll have to backtrack (or slash through the wilderness) to reach your destination. Cut your losses and move on.

What aspect of your book worries you the most? Do your first four chapters focus on a character who has begun to bore you, who doesn't appear at all in later scenes? Is there anything you're worried you might have to dump, not just a single scene, but a major plotline? Your novel's basic concept? What?

If you get rid of this part of your book, what will the effect be? What new thing will rise and take over the space left by the old thing you've removed?

"I type out beginnings and they're awful, more of an unconscious parody of my previous book than the breakaway from it that I want. I need something driving down the center of a book, a magnet to draw everything to it— that's what I look for during the first months of writing something new. I often have to write a hundred pages or more before there's a paragraph that's alive. Okay, I say to myself, that's your beginning, start there; that's the first paragraph of the book. I'll go over the first six months of work and underline in red a paragraph, a sentence, sometimes no more than a phrase, that has some life in it, and then I'll type all these out on one page. Usually it doesn't come to more than one page, but if I'm lucky, that's the start of page one. I look for the liveliness to set the tone. After the awful beginning come the months of freewheeling play, and after the play come the crises, turning against your material and hating the book." —*Philip Roth*

Words, Words, Words

This exercise is related to "Sentence Types" on pages 100–101—another mechanical rather than thematic exercise meant to help make choices regarding writing style. As you did in "Sentence Types," copy a paragraph of about ten sentences from a novel whose style you admire. Use a different book than you used for "Sentence Types."

Answer the following questions about your model paragraph.
- How many words of only one syllable are there in your paragraph? _____
- How many words with three or more syllables are there? _____
- How many pronouns? _____
- How many concrete nouns (things you can see, touch, smell, or hear, such as *partridge, England, sky, train*)? _____
- How many active verb constructions? ("Jasper *believes* that eating turkey cures jet lag" [Ann Hood, *Something Blue*].) _____
- How many passive verb constructions? ("By a strange quirk of fate, I *was brought* back by a memory" [Karen Tei Yamashita, *Through the Arc of the Rain Forest*]. "In babyhood and boyhood I *was called* Ambrose" [Edison Marshall, *The Pagan King*].) _____

Now copy a passage of ten sentences or so from your own novel.

Now answer the following questions about the passage from your novel.
- How many words of only one syllable are there in your paragraph? _____
- How many words with three or more syllables? _____
- How many pronouns? _____
- How many concrete nouns? _____
- How many active verb constructions? _____
- How many passive verb constructions? _____

Again, rewrite your paragraph to conform as closely as possible to your model.

Another way to do the exercise is, instead of copying a paragraph by a writer you admire, copy one by a writer you *don't* admire. Look carefully at that writer's style. Do you recognize pitfalls that have repelled you and that you want to avoid in your own style?

"I thought that real writers were not people like me. I thought they were Englishmen or Frenchmen or Russians. I thought you had to be full of high seriousness like T.S. Eliot." —*Max Apple*

A Voice Not Your Own

In novels written in dialect, it's easy to see how the voice of a character is different from the voice of the writer. But even in novels where the characters' voices are not as different from the writer's as, say, Huckleberry Finn's from Mark Twain's, or Hazel Motes' from Flannery O'Connor's, a writer can have fun creating a voice very different from her own.

Write a scene in which the unique, quirky voice of one of your characters is the focus—and make that voice different from your own and that of any other character. Dialect and foreign accent are one way to go, but you can also use striking syntax or diction to create your unusual voice. Evelyn Waugh uses all of these in this speech from *Decline and Fall*, when the leader of a Welsh band introduces himself.

> We are the silver band the Lord bless and keep you. . . . the band that no one could beat whatever but two indeed in the Eisteddfod that for all North Wales was look you.

"I've always been bored with my own autobiography, and I feel I have no accent anyone can identify. . . . *Autobiography of My Mother* is written in an accent almost wholly borrowed and fabricated. . . . The parameters of someone else's voice are clear to me; my own are not." —*Rosellen Brown*

Draw a Picture

Draw full-length, head-to-foot pictures of four or five of your main characters. Let them stand in a line next to one another so differences in their heights and weights will be apparent. Dress them in clothes typical of what they would wear on a given occasion—to a party, for example, or to work. If drawing isn't your talent, make notes to indicate important points that aren't completely clear—for example, if one character is wearing genuine Birkenstock sandals and another has on cheap imitations, or four-inch ankle straps, or Doc Martens, or really old flip-flops. Try to let the character's personality, as well as her economic situation, come through as much as possible through her hairstyle and dress. Colored pencils are a good choice for this exercise, or use a regular no. 2 pencil if you think you'll have to do a lot of erasing.

"A young student came to me who had been through a program of theology, so she was very heavily cerebral. She said she wanted to be a writer and showed me something she had written. I said, 'What are the people wearing?' and she said, 'I don't care.' I said, 'Unless you care, you're not going to be a writer.' You don't have to put all that stuff in the story, what they had for breakfast, what kind of socks they have on, but you have to know it, and not only that, you have to care enough about such details to pay attention to them. Paper dolls are useful in that respect."—*Margaret Atwood*

Take a Walk!

Take a few hours off to spend outside. You'll benefit psychically, and practically too, even if—maybe especially if—you don't have a particular destination or writing-related goal in view.

Go out with your notebook on a walk, take a bus, or get someone who promises not to talk for a few hours to drive you somewhere. Get as close to actual nature—growing things, few people—as you can. Ideally, find a place roughly equivalent to a place where your novel occurs, but one with which you aren't totally familiar: Your goal here is discovery. E.L. Doctorow, driving through the Adirondacks, imagined a setting and plot for his novel *Loon Lake* after by chance seeing a road sign for Loon Lake: "I imagined a private railroad train going through the forest. The train was taking a party of gangsters to the mountain retreat of a powerful man of great wealth. So there it was, a feeling for a place, an image or two, and I was off in pursuit of my book."

When you return, take some time to review your notes and to record as vividly as possible your impressions of what you have seen and done.

"One ought, every day at least, to hear a little song, read a good poem, see a fine picture, and, if it were possible, to speak a few reasonable words." —*Johann Wolfgang von Goethe*

Arbitrary Choices

If you're worried that your novel is becoming predictable, or if you're simply not sure what you should do next, do something that shakes up or undermines the ordinary, conscious writing process a little. William Burroughs determined the order of scenes in *Naked Lunch* by throwing his typescripts into the air. French writer Georges Perec's decision not to use the letter *e* in his 1969 novel, *A Void*, limited his palette, forcing him into decisions he would not have made if he had used the whole alphabet. (A 1995 English translation of *A Void* by Gilbert Adair also omits the *e*.)

Write a scene that depends on some element of chance for its creation. Force yourself, for example, to write a scene using the five words your finger falls on when you open the dictionary at random.

"All serious writers are interested in experimentation. It is a means by which they honor their craft."
—*Joyce Carol Oates*

Cubing

Cubing, a six-part exercise based on the sides of a cube, is designed to help writers examine ideas from different points of view, to overcome writer's block, and to become open to subtle ideas that their conscious minds might have blocked out.

First, decide what aspect of your novel you plan to explore in your cube. This could be a character, a particular chapter or scene, or a particular writing problem you're wrestling with. Then, using a timer, spend exactly five minutes writing a response to each of the six prompts below. Even if a particular "side" of the cube doesn't seem to relate to your novel, force yourself to write anyway. Your answers to the apparently irrelevant prompts will often be the most valuable. Don't stop writing even if you have no idea what you're going to say next. Write nonsense if you need to, but try to get back to your subject. Stop only briefly at the end of each response. Most people will end up with a couple of pages of writing.

Describe your subject. What does he/she/it look like?

Compare. What is it similar to? Different from?

Associate. What other things does your subject make you think of?

Analyze. Where did your subject come from? What is it doing now? Where is it going?

Apply. What is the purpose of your subject? What is its reason for existing?

Argue. What are some arguments in favor of your subject? Against it?

After you finish, reread what you've written. Highlight the passages that seem most important. Look for unexpected insights and striking turns of phrase. If you'd like, you can make a separate cube for each of your major characters or for each important scene.

"The business of the poet and novelist is to show the sorriness underlying the greatest things, and the grandness underlying the sorriest things." — *Thomas Hardy*

Collaboration

Ask someone to work with you to write a scene. You two can work side by side, with the other writer following strict guidelines you provide; or the other writer can work alone and then bring you a scene he has written, with his own suggestions for working it into the book. Writers are often solitary, but you might find working with someone else more useful than you'd think. Charles Dickens and Wilkie Collins collaborated on fiction, as did Joseph Conrad and Ford Madox Ford, who completed two novels in three years.

Your collaborator should be someone you get along with, but don't limit yourself to working with someone whose strengths are the same as your own. It might be useful to work with a poet, for example. If you don't know any other writers, pick any willing person who's familiar with your novel.

After you're finished, describe the experiment, what you learned from it, and how collaboration with another writer could help in the future. Did the results surprise you? Was it helpful to see a different view of your characters and plot? Did you choose a compatible writer to work with? Who else might you want to work with?

"Our synergy level peaking early, we arrange to be free from classes every day between 10:30 and 1:00. Perhaps this very brevity forces us to use our time efficiently. We write only on weekdays, but in our ten years of collaboration neither of us has ever missed a day because of illness or other commitments. We write forty-eight weeks a year, allowing two weeks at the end of each semester to recharge our individual batteries. This discipline has caused us at various times to write in homes, hospitals and airports." —*Hal Blythe and Charlie Sweet* (who do most of their collaborative writing at a McDonald's restaurant in Kentucky)

Do It in Your Head

Think of a short scene—a paragraph or so—that needs to be in your novel, and create it entirely in your head, perfecting it as much as possible. Memorizing every word may seem impossible, but come as close as you can. After you've developed your scene mentally, write it from memory. This exercise requires that you concentrate hard on individual word choice.

This activity can be especially useful if your real life is full of work that takes up a lot of time but leaves your mind free—if you're in a cotton mill all day, you can still be doing necessary thinking about your book. Writing in your head is liberating for some writers as well because it makes it easy to play around with ideas, even outrageous ones, without committing them to paper. In an interview, one of Vladimir Nabokov's editors reported that Nabokov had completed an entire novel in his head: "It's all there: the characters, the scenes, the details. He is about to do the actual writing on three-by-five-inch cards."

"I don't work in a continual manner at all, it's not possible. I believe I work twenty-four hours a day, but without writing. I write very little—what I mean is, when I write one page, when it comes, that's a lot. But that page, it's been four or five days in the works or six or eight months. I write in small chunks, but without leaving the book."
—*Edmond Jabès*

The Least Likely Thing

Think of the least likely action you can imagine any of your characters doing—and then make them do it. In Alice Adams' *Caroline's Daughters*, two sisters, rather snobbish and materialistic but not actually criminals, impulsively leave their current jobs to open a high-end house of prostitution. The act is surprising but not totally out of character. Your goal here is not to choose the silliest, most out-of-the-blue behavior possible, but to keep your characters from becoming boring and predictable, to let the reader get a new perspective on your characters' personalities so they will seem as rich and various as real people.

"It's easy to lose the energy that you need for a long piece unless the characters are surprising you and showing you something new every week or even every month or every other paragraph, however often it comes."
—*Alice McDermott*

Other People's Stories

If you've kept a writer's journal for long, it is probably full of stories you've heard from other people—gossip, amazing coincidences, jokes, and revelations. Whether your novel is autobiographical or not, consider including real events from other people's lives, especially if you've run out of stories from your own life, as a way of enriching your material.

Write a particularly memorable anecdote—a short, complete story told to make a point—that really occurred in someone else's life. Then consider how this anecdote might fit into your novel. Could it be an event from a character's past? A story related by a character in a confessional moment?

"We know about the people who walk into the police station and confess to crimes they haven't committed. Well, the false confession appeals to writers, too. Novelists are even interested in what happens to other people and, like liars and con men everywhere, will pretend that something dramatic or awful or hair-raising actually happened to them. The physical particulars and moral circumstances of Zuckerman's mother's death have practically nothing to do with the death of my own mother. The death of the mother of one of my dearest friends—whose account of her suffering stuck in my mind long after he'd told me about it—furnished the most telling details for the mother's death in *The Anatomy Lesson*."—*Philip Roth*

Mapping

Draw a map of some of the territory your novel covers. You can map a large area: the city where your characters live, for example. Who lives in the most desirable area of town? Who lives next to the toxic waste dump? What does the choice of suburbs vs. city say about your characters? Who is in position to spy into the kitchen window of another character?

On the other hand, your map might cover only a small space: the rooms of the house or apartment in which your characters live, perhaps. In any case, maps can help you see characters in their own spaces and can help you move your people around.

Here are two maps from Sir Arthur Conan Doyle's *The Return of Sherlock Holmes*. You might want to include your maps in your finished novel, or they can exist simply to help you imagine the place in your own mind.

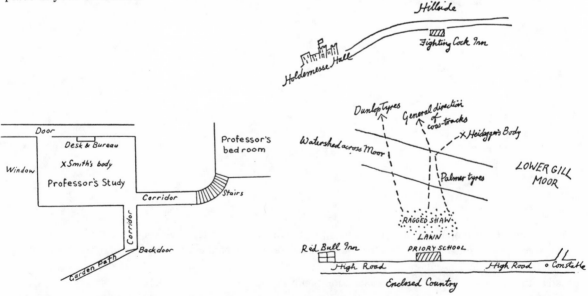

"If I had to teach a class on writing a novel, I would suggest writing the major point for each chapter on a card. Then, hang them up in order and write in the details. Of

Double-Checking and Revising

Hearing What You Write

Without an audience, read your favorite chapter aloud. Stop when something sounds wrong and mark suggestions for revision. After you're finished, look at the changes you made. Is there a pattern to the kind of revisions you marked? If you made a lot of significant changes to the manuscript, consider reading the entire novel aloud, as a revision tool.

Now think of a scene you haven't written yet. Instead of writing it, speak it into a tape recorder. Transcribe a couple of paragraphs from the tape below. Leave out the "uh's" and the "and-and's," and the "Oh, I forgot to say but this also happened's," but otherwise be as faithful to the tape as you can.

After you're done transcribing, review what you've written. Are the paragraphs you transcribed as good as—or less good than—your usual paragraphs? Might a tape recorder become one of your regular tools for writing?

"I would rather tell a story than have someone read it. I do a lot of reading. I was at Auburn in Montgomery this past weekend, and people there had read the stories—they had read *A Gathering of Old Men*, and yet they said, when you read it, I get something else out of it. I write to be read out loud, especially when I'm dealing with the first person point of view." —*Ernest J. Gaines*

Epigraphs

An epigraph is a quotation from another source—a book, a song—that appears at the beginning of your novel and indicates its theme in some way. Much of David Shields' *Dead Languages* concerns the protagonist's stammering; here's the epigraph (from Joseph Conrad's *Lord Jim*).

> Are not our lives too short for that full utterance which through all our stammerings is of course our only and abiding intention?

Find a passage that would make a suitable epigraph for your novel. If you can, come up with several possibilities. If your novel is divided into sections, you might want to have an epigraph at the beginning of each section.

SOME GUIDELINES:
- The epigraph shouldn't be too familiar. (In his book *Writing a Novel*, John Braine asserts that no writer should ever be allowed to pull an epigraph from *Hamlet* or *Macbeth*.)
- The epigraph should comment on the novel's theme in some way but not simply restate it.
- Ideally, the significance of the epigraph will not be completely understood until the end of the novel.

Remember that the epigraph doesn't have to be literary: It can be anything you choose.

"I don't look at my early drafts in hard copy. I just open another file in my word processor and start from scratch. Each draft helps me know my characters better; draft by draft, their voices get louder and they tell me their adventures more fully each time through. The characters thicken, becoming more dense and complex. I hear the sentences better. I do a lot of drafts. In order to get these very dense, high-energy sentences, I've thought through much bulkier paragraphs." —*Bharati Mukherjee*

Conflict for Everyone

Make a list of all of the named characters in your novel, and then, after the character's name, note what conflicts the character is involved in. One example is provided.

CHARACTER

Eustacia Vye, in Thomas Hardy's
The Return of the Native

CONFLICTS

conflict with husband, who wishes to stay on Egdon Heath; she wants to leave

conflict with mother-in-law, who accuses her of taking money meant for son and niece

Now pay special attention to the characters in the novel who are involved in no conflicts or only minor ones. Ask yourself, are they worth keeping? If you do have such characters, justify their continued existence in a paragraph or two.

"After five years at CNN, even though I loved the place, I was burned out and bitter. So I wrote my own book, set at the All News Network. It was very much a roman á clef. I killed off people I knew. It was a way for me to digest the experience." — *Sparkle Hayter*

Switch Your Point of View

Take a paragraph in which your protagonist appears and rewrite it using a different point of view. If your novel is in first person (for example, "When I was a young girl in China, my grandmother told me my mother was a ghost" [Amy Tan, *The Joy Luck Club*]), put it into third person. If it's in third person (for example, "She wore her newest clothes on singing days" [Muriel Spark, *The Prime of Miss Jean Brodie*]), change it to first person.

Remember that the third-person point of view is divided into several subcategories. Ask yourself how many characters' minds the reader can see into. If just one, then the point of view is considered limited omniscient; if the reader can see into more than one mind, the point of view is simply omniscient. It's also possible to write a novel from the "fly on the wall" point of view, in which you see into the minds of no characters and can know how people feel and what they're thinking only by the narrator's description of the characters' appearance and behavior.

Mary Gordon says that changing the point of view in *Final Payments* from third to first person "allowed Isabel to be more intimate and more self-exploratory. I had done an awful lot of rumination and I realized that the direction of the novel tended to be quite ruminative."

Big Rewriting

Consider your crisis points—moments of high tension in which the outcome of the events will substantially affect the lives of your characters—and imagine what would happen if these charged situations ended radically differently from the way they do now. In Gail Godwin's *The Odd Woman*, Jane, the graduate student protagonist, imagines what will happen if she spends the afternoon and evening with her hotel roommate rather than going out to a lecture.

> They would stay in this room, dredging up vulnerabilities, old grudges, new anxieties about jobs; they would console each other. Then they would probably go out to dinner together and, over a bottle of wine, each would convince herself she had found a dear friend. The next morning each would awake to find herself as separate as ever, and feel slightly hostile toward each other for the delusion brought on by the weakness of the day before.

At the lecture she attends rather than spending time with her roommate, Jane meets the married man who becomes her lover.

On the lines below, list the main crisis points in your novel, and then describe what would happen if the crisis were resolved differently—totally opposite from the way it does now, if possible. Then ask yourself, is the new way better?

CRISIS   **OPPOSITE OUTCOME**

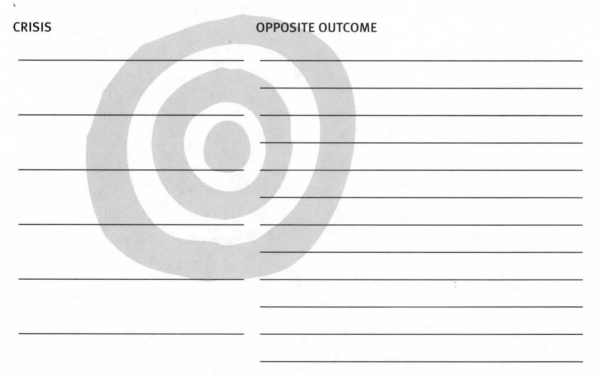

Novelist Larry Brown rewrote the ending of *Joe* five times: "One was a happily-ever-after where everything was hunky-dory. But the question that I ultimately had to ask myself was: Do the guilty always get punished in life, or do the innocent sometimes have to catch some stuff? And I said, in the real world they do, and if your fiction really imitates life, that's what you have to go with. I build my stories, and I try to be authentic in them."

Is This Scene Necessary?

A scene is a dramatized event, usually involving detailed description and dialogue, that occurs over the course of an unbroken stretch of time. Most novels are a combination of scene and summary (in which an event is described but not dramatized). Often, a writer will make scenes out of the most interesting, dramatic, or exciting events of a novel and summarize the others. After you have been working for at least a few months, list the scenes you've written so far. Then, after each scene, describe its function. What does each scene contribute to your novel?

The word *scene* in fiction is more related to time than to place. In the first chapter of Louise Erdrich's *Love Medicine*, for example, June Kapshaw, "a long-legged Chippewa woman, aged hard in every way except how she moved," has been waiting for a bus to take her from a North Dakota town to her reservation home. On a whim, she picks up a stranger in a bar, finally ending up in his truck. After the man falls asleep, June starts walking back to town. Nearly there, she changes her mind and instead heads toward the reservation, an impossibly long trip on which she freezes to death. The characters move around a lot in this chapter, but because there is no break in the time continuum, the chapter remains a single scene.

SCENE   FUNCTION

_____   _____

_____   _____

_____   _____

_____   _____

_____   _____

_____   _____

_____   _____

"The most important lesson in the writing trade is that any manuscript is improved if you cut away the fat."
—*Robert Heinlein*

The Most Important Scene

Is there a scene you haven't written yet, either because you're not sure what's going to happen or perhaps because it's the climactic scene and if you mess up on that one, the whole novel will fail? Then write the scene. Don't worry if it sounds good, if it's embarrassing, or even if everything in it makes sense. You can revise later. The important thing is to get it down on paper, because if you don't you'll never finish your novel.

Francine du Plessix Gray, who writes a minimum of four drafts of her fiction, says, "The first thing we must do when we set out to write . . . is to shed all narcissism. My own decades of fear came from my anxiety that my early drafts were ugly, sloppy, not promising enough. We must persevere and scrawl atrocities, persevere dreadful draft after dreadful draft in an unhindered stream of consciousness, persevere, if need be, in Breton's technique of automatic writing, of mindless trance. And within that morass of words there may be an ironic turn of phrase, a dislocation that gives us a key to the voice, the tone, the structure we're struggling to find."

"They can't yank a novelist like they can a pitcher. A novelist has to go the full nine, even if it kills him."

—*Ernest Hemingway*

Chopping Up a Long Scene

Turn to the longest scene you've written and count the pages. Especially if this scene is more than a page or two longer than your other scenes, ask yourself if perhaps you should break up the long scene, to avoid disrupting the rhythm of your novel. This is what Scott Turow did in *Presumed Innocent*, when his editor suggested that Turow divide a chapter "describing Rusty's past relationship with Carolyn" into three separate chapters, "interspersing it because it was a hard gulp."

As an exercise (you can always change your mind), break your longest scene into two or more shorter ones, each separated by at least one other scene. Describe the changes you might make. Where will the breaks occur? Where will the new, shorter scenes be placed? Will you need to write transitional passages in order for the new scenes to fit gracefully where you place them?

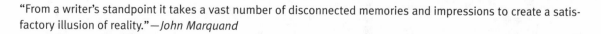

"From a writer's standpoint it takes a vast number of disconnected memories and impressions to create a satisfactory illusion of reality." —*John Marquand*

Sharing Your Work

Ask someone you trust to read what you've written so far and comment on it. Having another writer as a reader might be particularly helpful; on the other hand, it might be useful to choose someone you think of as the typical—or ideal—reader of your novel. If you're writing a romance, for example, it might be useful to choose someone who reads a lot of romances. Use the following questionnaire as a guide, and add relevant questions of your own to make your reader's responses more helpful.

If you *really* trust your reader, ask him to write a response to your work here. If you'd prefer that your reader not read other entries in this book, note the gist of your reader's comments yourself.

Who do you think is the most interesting character? Why?

Were there important characters who didn't interest you, who perhaps seemed stereotypical or boring?

At what point did you find yourself most caught up in the action? Why?

Were there any passages that seemed to drag a bit? On the other hand, were there places where you felt things were happening too fast?

Which part was the most humorous? Which part was the saddest? Did you laugh at places I didn't mean to be funny?

Were there places where you didn't quite understand what was going on? Or were there places where the events of the plot didn't seem to follow logically?

Did you find grammatical errors, lapses in connection, or annoying style tics?

Did the ending seem right?

Were there any aspects that I meant as a surprise that seemed overly predictable?

Was there anything that you wanted to learn about but never did? Were all the loose ends tied up?

Where did you find the language of the writing the most beautiful?

Were there places where the description seemed clichéd?

Is there anything else you'd like to add?

Saul Bellow comments, "George Sand wrote to Flaubert, in a collection of letters I looked into the other day, that she hoped he would bring his copy of her latest book on his next visit. 'Put in it all the criticisms which occur to you,' she said. 'That will be very good for me. People ought to do that for each other as Balzac and I used to do. That doesn't make one person alter the other; quite the contrary, for in general one gets more determined in one's *moi*, one completes it, explains it better, entirely develops it, and that is why friendship is good, even in literature, where the first condition of any worth is to be one's self.' How nice it would be to hear this from a writer. Writers today seldom wish each other well."

Bad Advice

A rejection slip for George Orwell's *Animal Farm* is said to read, "It is impossible to sell animal stories in the U.S.A." Let's hope Orwell was later able to laugh. Very likely you too have been given counsel about your writing, some of which turned out to be bad. Write all the pieces of bad advice you can remember ever receiving about your writing.

ADVICE	FROM WHOM?	WHY BAD?
Make protagonist more sympathetic.	Many classmates at college	The protagonist would become boring; also, his reform is a big part of the plot, so he must be bad at first.

Of course, it's possible that the advice you initially think is bad may actually be good and you just don't want to face it. Do you note patterns in the advice you've received? Write some words of advice you've received that at first seemed incorrect but later seemed justified.

"During part of the time I was writing *The Folded Leaf*, I was in analysis with Theodor Reik, who thought the book ought to have a positive ending. And Edward Aswell at *Harper's* thought the story would be strengthened if I combined some of the minor characters. I was so tired and unconfident about the book that I took their word for it. Later I was sorry." — *William Maxwell*

When It's Going *Too* Well

Reread the scene of your novel that you wrote the fastest, that came the most easily, the one you found the least need to revise. Does it still look great, perhaps because you were unusually inspired when you wrote it? Or did it come quickly because you weren't thinking enough, because you were willing, for example, to settle for clichés? Philip Roth has said, "Fluency can be a sign that nothing is happening, fluency can actually be my signal to stop, while being in the dark from sentence to sentence is what convinces me to go on."

Read your quickly written scene aloud, marking any awkward spots as you go. Then, without looking at the scene, try to recreate it. Compare the two versions. Which is better? Is the original version still satisfying, or is something missing?

"Every day when I get up and look at what I've done the day before, I try to eliminate what I used to call 'he said, she said writing.' The dead circumstantial. I replace scenes in which things simply happen with language as vivid as I can make it, with ellipsis, metaphor, summary which makes a pattern, something which distinguishes the writing from the plodding prose one often finds in realistic fiction." — *Rosellen Brown*

How Invisible Are You?

For most writers, getting the reader caught up in the story is the whole point. In an interview, Joyce Carol Oates remarks, "Most artists, and certainly the writer, aspire to invisibility by way of art. . . . Most novelists—though not of course all—really do attempt to refine themselves out of existence by way of an immersion, a systematic and disciplined immersion, in language."

Some writers, though, play with the reader by reminding her frequently that she is reading a work of fiction, not an exact replica of real life. Within the text of *The French Lieutenant's Woman*, John Fowles admits that he really does not know why he has caused his character Sarah to contemplate suicide on a window ledge. "I do not know," he says. "This story I am telling is all imagination. These characters I create never existed outside my own mind."

If your goal, like Oates', is to be as invisible as possible, write a paragraph in which you do the opposite. Jar the surface of your chapter. Make it clear that your novel is fiction and not a replication of real life. Step in, as Fowles does, and comment on the novel's events so far. Or add footnotes, as Nicholson Baker does in *The Mezzanine*. Or break up the text with unusual spacing or typefaces, as Donald Barthelme and James Joyce have done.

On the other hand, if you *want* the reader to keep in mind that she is reading a novel, if you want to keep the reader from becoming lost in the fictional dream, take a half hour or so and write a few paragraphs that seem completely realistic, in which you, as the novelist, become as imperceptible as possible.

"I have enough of the postmodernist in me—although I hope that I'm on the humorous wing of postmodernism—to want to remind the reader that it is no use getting het-up about a character, since the character is only there to serve this fiction."—*Martin Amis*

Mincing Words

Even if your writing style tends to be lushly descriptive—and you like that—rewrite one of your scenes, omitting as much description, stage direction, and dialogue as you possibly can without losing anything vital. How much can you leave out? Half? A third? What does the scene gain, if anything, from brevity? Might you consider being a bit more terse in future scenes?

This short passage from Fay Weldon's *Remember Me* comes fairly early in the novel, after Hilary's stepmother has impulsively taken her out of school to get a haircut.

> Hilary, horrified by her appearance, leaves the hairdresser in tears. Lily is irritated by this display of ingratitude; what is more, she is landed with Hilary for the rest of the day, for Hilary refuses to return to school. Not only will it be quite obvious to everyone that she has been to the hairdresser, and not to the dentist, but how can she face her classmates looking such a freak?

Note how Weldon has been able to succinctly convey the teenage Hilary's anguish, the stepmother's exasperation, and the bad relationship between the characters, with virtually no physical description or conversation. We never get a real picture of Hilary's bad haircut, but it's not the actual hairstyle that matters.

"To write simply is as difficult as to be good."—*Somerset Maugham*

Comedy or Tragedy?

On a scale from one to ten, rank how happily you plan to end your novel.

1. utter dispair
2. Hamlet
3. brutal realism
4. just a touch of hope
5. comme çi, comme ça

6. silver lining to some clouds
7. supper's cooked, the car runs
8. no clouds
9. cures discovered to most diseases
10. no death; love and good jobs for all

Describe the choices you made, consciously or subconsciously, that led you to this decision to end your novel tragically or happily.

Now suppose that the fiction god held a thunderbolt to your head and told you to move your novel at least two levels to the right or left. If you ranked your conclusion a six in the happiness category, for example, what would have to change in your plot for the novel to become a four or an eight?

"It's much easier to write a solemn book than a funny book. It's harder to make people laugh than it is to make them cry. People are always on the verge of tears." — *Fran Lebowitz*

Really Ending

You've probably faced the fact that your book is going to take a long time to complete. Herman Wouk wrote in his journal on May 17, 1962, "I may as well start my task. . . . I am entering on a work that can hardly take me less than three years." He did not reach the conclusion of his novel, however, until June 4, 1978.

Still, it wouldn't be productive to work on the same novel for the rest of your life. Write a wish list of what you need in order to finish. More ideas? More writing time? Some idea of what you'll do after you've finished the book?

Then write what you can do to acquire whatever you need to finish the book. Finally, set a realistic—but not too distant—goal for completion.

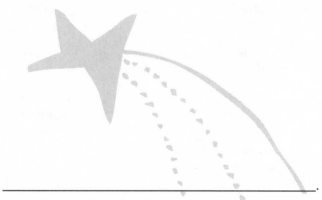

I plan to finish my novel on or before (date) _____.

Asked, "How do you know when you've reached the end with each book?" novelist Brion Gysin replied, "I never knew. It's never the end. It's the end of the book; that is, it's always unfinished, but it's where I feel I cannot go on anymore. I feel it."

Copyediting and Proofreading

At some point, but typically after you've completed what seem to be your final revisions, you're going to want to look at some mechanical aspects of the novel that you may well have ignored during the early part of the writing process. If you can get someone with a sharp eye to proofread as well, that's great, but you should also do it yourself, since you know better than anyone what to look for. Here is a checklist of some typical bugbears.

_____ Have I made spelling and typographical errors? Read your novel with a big dictionary beside you. Run the spell checker if you're on the computer, but don't trust it to do all of your work; remember homonyms, omitted words, and so on.

_____ Are my margins, type fonts, line spacing (double-spaced is best), and number of spaces per paragraph indentation consistent from chapter to chapter?

_____ Are my pages numbered consecutively, with the page number appearing at the same place on each page?

_____ Are the chapters numbered consistently? (Don't give some titles roman numerals and some Arabic numerals.) If the chapters are titled, does each chapter have a title?

_____ Are there errors in continuity? Do any of my characters' names change from chapter to chapter? Are character and place names spelled the same each time they appear?

_____ Are my grammar and punctuation good? If I tend to make apostrophe errors or subject-verb agreement errors, have I looked closely at those spots in particular?

_____ Do I use slang terms or other topical references that might appear dated or need to be explained later? A paragraph describing a character's envy of Princess Diana might be problematic in a novel set after the princess' death.

_____ Have I repeated myself unintentionally? Is a character's tasteless joke, meant to show his insensitivity, recounted completely more than once in the novel?

_____ Have I researched sufficiently any facts or details about subjects that aren't perfectly familiar to me already?

_____ Are any of my stylistic tics likely to annoy? For example, am I using synonyms for *said*, such as *responded*, *replied*, *announced*, *stated*, *commented*, *uttered*, and *spoke* so often that these words become noticeable and bothersome? Does the word really appear more than four times on most pages?

_____ Has my printer let me down? Are there blank pages in the middle of the manuscript?

_____ Have I used unnecessary computer tools? It's not a good idea to justify your type or use unusual typefaces (for example, Impact or Comic Sans MS) or the automatic hyphenation feature.

_____ Have I obtained all the things I need to make my manuscript look as good as possible:

     _____ word processor (or a good-quality electronic or electric typewriter, or a trust-worthy typist)?

     _____ sufficient toner cartridges or other ink to print the manuscript, including drafts?

     _____ enough paper (a box of ten reams of photocopy paper is a good idea; it's cheap, and you won't need to worry—for a while—about running out)?

List what you need to do before producing a perfect copy of your manuscript you'll be ready to show to others with reasonable pride. Then, check them off as you complete them.

Insufficient attention to detail in proofreading is bad, but it's worse to lose your manuscript altogether. You may know the story of Hadley Hemingway's loss of her husband's book manuscript on a European train. Don't let this happen to you! Novelist Carolyn Chute and her writer friends exchange manuscripts, which they call "fire books," as a method of protection. You might want to do this—or at least to keep a copy of a regularly updated computer disk in a safe place away from other copies of your manuscript, just in case. On the line below, write what you have done to prevent your manuscript from loss through fire, computer failure, carelessness, destruction by a for-mer loved one, or other catastrophes.

A copy of my manuscript (or a diskette) can be found _____.

The Next One

List the best ideas you've had since you've started this novel that just don't belong in the one you're working on now. Are there characters who no longer seem relevant but who are too good to jettison completely? Have you established the father-in-law's basement stash of plutonium plausibly and compellingly—and perhaps spent hours of research to learn what effects a box of plutonium in the basement would have on those living in the house—but finally realized there's no place for plutonium in your present book?

You can save those promising ideas for the next novel. Especially if you're writing a mystery, ask yourself also, does this novel deserve a sequel?

"Every book is a brand new adventure and I always go back to what Eudora Welty said, which is, every book teaches you the lessons necessary to write that book. The down side is that none of the lessons from one book have anything to do with the lessons I need to learn for the next, so, while in some sense of the word, thirty years of writing has served me well, there is a sense in which every time I go up to bat it's a brand new game and each time out, you know—and I'm sure this is true of other writers, too—you give away everything you have."

—Sue Grafton